INDIAN FICTION IN ENGLISH

Problems and Promises

Edited by

R. S. PATHAK

NORTHERN BOOK CENTRE
NEW DELHI

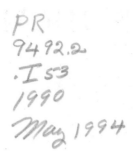

PR
9492.2
.I 53
1990
May 1994

ISBN 81-85119-86-4

Published under the authority of
Dr Harisingh Gour Vishwavidyalaya, Sagar.

Price

Published by Northern Book Centre, 4221/1, Ansari Road, Daryaganj, New Delhi-110 002.

Printed at Swatantra Bharat Press, 423, Gali Jainyan, Esplanade Road, Delhi-110 006.

CONTRIBUTORS

1. Dr R.C. Shukla is Principal, Government Girls' College, Chhindwara, Madhya Pradesh.

2. Dr S.C. Dwivedi teaches at Allahabad University, Allahabad.

3. Dr H.S.S. Bais is Reader in English at Dr H.S. Gour Vishwavidyalaya, Sagar.

4. Dr (Mrs) S. Sengupta teaches at Dr H.S. Gour Vishwavidyalaya, Sagar.

5. Dr K.K. Sharma is Professor of English at Allahabad University, Allahabad.

6. Dr (Mrs) S. Sivaraman is Reader in English, Dr H.S. Gour Vishwavidyalaya, Sagar.

7. Mr Sunil Kumar teaches at Dr H.S. Gour Vishwavidyalaya, Sagar,

8. Dr C. Sengupta is Reader in English at Dr H.S. Gour Vishwavidyalaya, Sagar.

9. Miss Mridula Bajpai was associated with the Department of English at Dr H.S. Gour Vishwavidyalaya, Sagar, as a Ph.D. research scholar and an *ad hoc* Lecturer. Now in Indian Civil Services.

10. Dr (Mrs) Urmila Varma is Reader in English at Dr H.S. Gour Vishwavidyalaya, Sagar.

11. Dr A.N. Dwivedi is Reader in English at Allahabad University, Allahabad.

12. Mr S.M. Khanna teaches English at Government P.G. College, Tikamgarh, Madhya Pradesh.

13. Dr O.P. Mathur was formerly Professor and Head of the Department of English at B.H.U., Varanasi.

14. Dr A.K. Awasthi is Reader at Dr H.S. Gour Vishwavidyalaya, Sagar.

15. Dr R.S. Pathak is Professor and Head of the Department of English and Other European Languages, Dr Harisingh Gour Vishwavidyalaya, Sagar.

16. Dr R.P. Tewari is Professor and Head of the Department of English, R.B.S. College, Agra.

17. Dr O.P. Bhatnagar is Professor of English at Vidarbh Mahavidyalaya, Amravati. He is a well-known poet and critic.

PREFACE

The Indian novel in English owed its inception to India's contact with the Western mind. The unprecedented awakening transformed the general outlook and resulted in the Renaissance, which is said to be the greatest gift of the English to India. Ever since the publication of Bankim Chandra Chatterjee's novel *Rajmohan's Wife* in 1864, Indian fiction in English has grown considerably in bulk, variety and maturity. Its development can be traced from its imitative and experimental stage to realistic to psychological. The verve and resilience of the Indian novel in English, notwithstanding all its limitations, are undeniable and, as Mulk Raj Anand says, it has 'come to stay as part of world literature'.

On account of historical reasons, however, the Indian novelist in English has to face various challenges. For example, he has to seek and assert his identity. Then, he has to forge a suitable medium for self-expression. Both these issues bristle with endless difficulties. Some of the main problems, trials and tribulations of the Indian novel in English along with its promises have been discussed in the present volume. Although there is no dearth of anthologies of critical essays on Indian Writing in English, its fiction has not been considered from this point of view with the same amount of thoroughness and sense of urgency.

The essays in this volume were originally presented at an All-India Seminar organized by the Department of English and Other European Languages, Dr Harisingh Gour Vishwavidyalaya, Sagar, in January 1988. I am extremely grateful to all the distinguished contributors who so readily responded to our invitation. Some of them even revised the earlier draft of their papers for the present volume. The organization of the Seminar was made possible by a grant made available to us by the University. I am personally grateful to all those persons who have been kind enough to extend their unstinted help, affectionate encouragement and valuable advice, but for which the present volume would not have assumed the present shape.

Sagar
10 February 1990   R.S. PATHAK

CONTENTS

CONTENTS

Introduction

The Indian fiction in English is now a living, developing and evolving literary genre. It is being accepted as a signi ficant part of Commonwealth Literature. Although the Indian novel in English began as a 'hot-house plant', it has taken firm roots in the Indian soil. In recent decades, it has acquired a distinct significance in the context of the contemporary Indian literary scene. For a proper understanding of India's literary achievements and socio-cultural milieu, its importance can hardly be overstated.

Indian Writing in English has been described as 'a Janus-faced literature' born of 'a cross-fertilization of two faithful cultures'—Indian and European.[1] The contact with the Western mind stirred the soul of India, ushering in the Renaissance which is said to be 'the greatest gift of the English' to India.[2] It gave rise to an unprecedented awakening and kindled new aspirations. A climate, pregnant with unforeseen possibilities, transformed the general outlook and a new literature emerged.

The earliest contacts of Indians with the English can be traced back to 31 December 1600, when Queen Elizabeth I granted a charter to a few merchants of London giving them the monopoly of trade with India and East. The activities of the Missionaries, which started in 1614 with permission to use the East India Company's ships may also be mentioned in this context, Except between 1698 and 1765, when encouragement to them declined, their educational activities continued unabated specially in the States of Bengal, Bombay and Madras.[3] These contacts, however, did not have a pervasive impact.

Precisely speaking, the story of English education in India dates back to 7 March 1835 when the Governor-General, Lord William Bentinck, resolved :

The great object of the British Government ought to be promotion of European literature and science among the natives of India, and all funds appropriated for the purpose of education would be best employed on English education alone.

With this resolution, the stamp of authority was affixed on the anglicization of the educated classes in this country. This administrative decision was, in fact, the culmination of a social movement at the head of which stood Raja Rammohan Roy, a Titan among men.

The Renaissance in India can be said to have actually started when the Hindu College of Calcutta (later known as the Presidency College) was established in 1817. It may be recalled that Warren Hastings had already established the Calcutta Medarassa in 1781 and that Sir William Jones had organized the Royal Society of Bengal in 1784. The process of anglicization of Indians was accelerated by Lord Macaulay's efforts to create a class of persons through English education who would be "Indian in blood and colour but English in taste, in opinion, in morals and intellect". He was not sure if such a day would ever come. But "whenever it comes", he added, "it will be the proudest day in English history" and the Empire would be "the imperishable empire of our arts and our morals, our literature and our laws."[4] Lord Hastings's Resolution of 1844 and the Wood Despatch of 1854 decisively established the teaching of English in India, which ultimately resulted in the creation of that 'dominant minority'[5] of Indian society which can be credited with the inception of Indian Writing in English.

Ever since the publication of Bankim Chandra Chatterjee's novel *Rajmohan's Wife* in 1864, Indian fiction in English has grown considerably in bulk, variety and maturity. Its development can be traced from its imitative and experimental stage to realistic to psychological. It was only in the 1920s that the Indian novel in English began to carve out its identity. After World War I it became determinedly more realistic and less idealized. It made deliberate efforts to depict the distress of the downtrodden classes, portraying India as she really is, 'warts and all', The novels written between the two World Wars were chiefly concerned with the social milieu, as is evident from representative works of the period like Mulk Raj Anand's *Untouchable* (1935), R.K. Narayan's *Swami and Friends* (1935) and Raja Rao's *Kanthapura* (1938). The novel proved valuable to the nationalists and revolutionaries as a convenient means of popularizing their cause. The surging nationalistic feelings were such that the scene ''shifted to the contemporary battles and agitations.''[6]

After 1950s, however, the interest of Indian novelists in English shifted from the public to the private sphere. They began to delineate the individual's quest for the self in all its varied and complex forms and his problems and crises. In their search for new themes, the novelists ''renounced the larger world in favour of the inner man'' and engaged themselves in ''a search for the essence of human living.''[7] As is evident from certain recent works, it contains seeds of future developments. A harvest of new talents has already altered the picture of Indian literature in English and, as Mulk Raj Anand says, it has 'come to stay as part of world literature'.[8] It has caught the attention of readers and critics all over the world.

When Indian Writing in English started appearing, it was not taken seriously. Gordon Bottomley described it as 'Matthew Arnold in a *saree*'. Even Indians were not very optimistic about the achievements of this literature. Uma Parameshwaran, for example, thinks that Indian literature in English, when compared to classical and vernacular literatures seems 'immature and insignificant' and that its 'future appears bleak, offering little but the prospect of extinction.' She categorically affirms that 'Indo-English literature seems destined to die young' and concludes : ''I set A D. 2000 as the dirge date for Indo-English literature'.[8] Fortunately, time has already proved this prediction wrong. Indian Writing in English has taken remarkable strides and has emerged as an acceptable body of writings of acknowledged worth. As David McCutchion points out, ''By a strange irony, Indian literature in English has been flourishing since

Independence more successfully than it ever flourished before."[9] The true potential of this literature can be appreciated if one compares the early novels in English written by Indians with the recent arrivals in the same field of literary creation.

Most early novels in English by Indians were immature and imitative. The literary scene before 1934—before Mulk Raj Anand, R.K. Narayan and Raja Rao published their first novels—was undoubtedly bleak. Tracing the growth of the Indian novel in English, Bhupal Singh wrote of the early works that they 'do not compare favourably' with the works produced by the English writers writing on the same or similar themes. He comments :

> That they write in a foreign tongue is a serious handicap in itself. Then few of them possess any knowledge of the art of fiction ; they do not seem to realise that prose fiction, in spite of its freedom, is subject to definite laws. In plot construction they are weak, and in characterisation weaker still. Their leaning towards didacticism and allegory is further obstacle to their success as novelists.[10]

During the past fifty years, Indian novelists in English have learnt much and their works have grown more authentic and varied.

The Indian novels in English are by all means worthy of our consideration. It is gratifying to note that the 'Big Three'—Anand, Narayan and Raja Rao—have lost none of their distinctive appeal. Among the novelists of the second generation, Kamala Markandaya, Manohar Malgonkar, Bhabani Bhattacharya and others have added new dimensions to this kind of writing. The novels of Anita Desai, Arun Joshi, Chaman Nahal, Salman Rushdie and others represent tremendous improvement upon the works of their predecessors. Talking of modern Indian novel in English, Anita Desai told an interviewer : "There is so little of it. ...There simply isn't enough, in the name of variety, value, interest, [and] significance."[11] If we compare Indian novels in English with those published in the Western world, they definitely appear insignificant and meagre in terms of both quantity and quality. But there are now more novels in English written by Indians than there used to be some three decades ago and their quality has gone up considerably.

Despite all gloomy forebodings, the Indian novel in English has come to stay with all its verve and resilience. It has received international attention, as would be evident if we pay attention to certain major literary events of the 1980s alone. The American Academy and Institute of Arts and Letters conferred an honorary membership on R. K. Narayan on 18 January 1982. He is the first Indian to receive this rare distinction. Salman Rushdie's novel *Midnight's Children* received a wide acclaim and won the coveted Booker Award for the year 1981. As a reviewer of *New York Times* put it, the novel "sounds like a continent finding its voice." The 446-page novel is set on an epic scale and encapsulates, in more than three-hundred-and-fifty thousand words, the panorama of Indian history before and after the partition.

The reception accorded to Venkatesh Kulkarni's *Naked in Deccan* also provides an unequivocal answer to those who predicted the death of the Indian fiction in English. For its literary excellence, Kulkarni's novel was awarded BCF American Book Award. The novel's fresh and original approach made it a best-seller, and its writer has been compared with Ignazio Silone and Gabriel Garcia Marquez. The novel deals with the multi-dimensional complexities of India and probes into them with searching philosophical intensity. For *Rich Like Us*, Nayantara Sahgal was awarded the Sinclair Prize for fiction in 1985. More recently, Nina Sibal's novel *Yatra* (1987) has won the International Grand Prix for Literature. The novel is an excellent attempt at presenting the scarred psyche of a violence-spattered nation. Bharati Mukherjee has been awarded the National Book Critics Circle (NBCC) Award for 1988 for her work *The Middleman and Other Stories*. Bharati Mukherjee is a "new voice" that has "added a brilliant chapter to the ongoing pageant of writing about the immigrant experience in America." What appealed to the members of NBCC was the books "humour, raciness and pathos." Mukherjee has published two novels—*The Tiger's Daughter* (1971) and *The Tiger's Daughter and Wife* (1975) and has just completed *Jasmine*. Moreover, in recent decades, some Indian writers including Mulk Raj Anand, R.K. Narayan, Anita Desai, Ved Mehta and G.V. Desani, have been published by the Penguin, the most prestigious paperbacks publishing house in the entire English-speaking world. These facts highlight a renewed interest on the part of the Western world in the Indian fiction in English.

The fecundity of modern Indian novel in English has been creditable. Its abundant variety, despite its limitations, both in respect of technique and subject-matter, can hardly be ignored. In 1980s alone, quite a few meritorious novels have been published. The most prominent among them are : R.K. Narayan, *A Tiger for Malgudi* (1983), Raja Rao, *The Chessmaster and his Moves* (1988), Arun Joshi, *The Last Labyrinth* (1981), Manohar Malgonkar, *Bendicoot Run* (1982) and *The Garland Keepers* (1986), Anita Desai *The Village by the Sea* (1982), *In Custody* (1984) and *Baumgartner's Bombay* (1988), Nayantara Sahgal, *Rich Like Us* (1985) and *Plans for Departure* (1986), Shashi Deshpande, *Come Up and Be Dead* (1983), Kamala Markandaya. *Pleasure City* (1982), K.D. Khosla, *Never the Twain* (1981), Gopalan, *Tryst with Destiny* (1981), V.A. Shahne, *Prajapati* (1984) and *Doctor Fauste* (1986), Amitav Ghosh, *The Circle of Reason* (1986), Salman Rushdie, *Shame* (1983) and the Whitebread Award-winning *Satanic Verses* (1988), Dina Mehta, *The Other Woman* (1981) and so on. Recently, Vikram Seth's verse novel, *The Golden Gate*, has been awarded the Sahitya Akademi Award. All these novels mark a distinct progression both in theme and technique. They seek to unfold Indian psyche through their innovative technique and demonstrate the resilience and vitality of the Indian novel in English. And as Anita Desai herself remarks, "It is depth which is interesting, delving deeper and deeper in character, a situation, or a scene rather than going about it."[12] At least some leading Indian novelists have tried their best to probe deeper into the recesses of human nature and delineate themes of wider appeal.

On account of historical reasons, however, the Indian novelists in English have to face unprecedented problems and challenges. They succeeded, where they did, by their enormous self-sacrifice. As C.D. Narasimhaiah remarks, creative writing in English and "intelligent response to our own writing [in it] has brought to the surface problems no one had suspected in our dealings with English litera-ture."[13] Writing in an adopted language—and writing successfully in it—is like walking on the razor's edge. "The problem of the choice of a subject," Iyengar points out, "the choice of the medium, [and] the choice of the technique...bristles with endless difficulties."[14] Unless the creative Indian writer in English is aware of these challen-ges and sorts them out satisfactorily, he cannot make any precise contribution.

The first and foremost problem that the Indian novelist in English has to face pertains to the quest and assertion of his identity. Victor Anant has analysed the predicament of a typical Indian in some detail. He draws attention to what he calls the 'mental slovenliness' and 'the emptiness of a hypnotised people,' who at the time of Independence were nothing different from 'a shuffling sleep-walking mass.' Most Indian writers, to him, are 'homeless orphans...child-ren of conflict, born in transit...[who live] smugly and comfortably on the borderline, battening on the profits that derive from playing the role of cultural schizophre-nic."[15] Edward Shil has also discussed the confusion and predicament of Indian writers in English. He endorses 'the common contention' that these writers are 'neurotic, schizophrenic, ambivalent, suspended between two worlds and rooted in neither.'[16] The greatest challenge before the Indian novelist in English is thus to seek and assert his identity. The displaced person's search for identity is a commonplace theme in modern fiction, but for most Indian novelists in English the quest 'has a peculiarly Indian immediacy.'[17] Although the problem of the Indian novelist may not be as acute as that of his counterpart in the Western world, his reiterative treatment of alienation, his persistent delineation of rootless characters and an awareness of his unfortunate predicament are symptomatic of his own problems.[18]

While seeking his individual identity, a writer forges his national identity also. The quest for identity in a country like India, unlike that in the West, is more socially oriented and less personal. Here the sense of individual coalesces with that of the nation and the individual quest becomes a microcosm for the national identity crisis. The real problem props up when an author tends to forget this fact. Then he would become, as Iyengar points out, 'a confused wanderer between the two worlds'—Indian and European.[19] It was probably this consideration which led Edmund Gosse to advise Sarojini Naidu to reveal 'the heart of India' in her writings by being 'a genuine poet of the Deccan, [and] not a clever machine-made imitation of the English classics.' The search for identity has taken two main directions—philosophical and sociological—in Indian fiction in English, represented by Raja Rao and Kamala Markandaya respectively. Most Indian novelists in English, however, seem to lack sufficient tenacity to pursue the quest for identity to its natural conclusion. They could not fully assert their identity forcefully chiefly because they were wholly unprepared for the shock of self-recogntion. Their sentimentality, window-dressing and nostalgia bordering on cumbersome confusion have acted like insuperable barriers to their recognition and affirmation of their individual and national identity.

As Donald Oken suggests, the loss of identity may result in alienation.[20] Alienation or rootlessness is a recurrent theme in Indian novels written in English. It is the dominant trait of several characters created by them, Meenakshi Mukherji writes that alienation is 'a very common theme' in the Indian novels in English.[21] Pritish Nandy also finds in them specimens of "a rootless literature, totally alienated from the people, unconcerned with Indian realities."[22] It is difficult to realise adequately the magnitude of the problem arising out of alienation unless we bear in mind that it is in the centre of all problems. It would be interesting, says Melwani, to investigate how far alienation as delineated in Indian novels in English is genuine and how far it is fad or fiction.[23] Quite a few Indian writers in English nevertheless do behave as literary outcasts. Nirad Choudhari has described himself as 'a nomad of the industrial age.'[24] He is not the only one betraying his roots. Many other writers also feel alienated in their home for one reason or another.

Another besetting problem that the Indian novelist in English has to face pertains to the medium of expression. He has to write in a language that is not his mother tongue. It has been pointed out repeatedly that a really excellent creative literature can be produced only in one's mother tongue. "An unfriendly spirit", writes Kantak, "hovers all our creative writing in an alien language."[25] Some people also feel that the creative writer has to grapple with a constant tension between the native sensibility and the acquired medium. Very few persons have appreciated the dilemma faced in respect of medium better than Raja Rao, himself a very competent Indian novelist in English. In his Foreward to *Kanthapura* he remarks : 'One has to convey in a language that is not one's own the spirit that is one's own. One has to convey the various shades and omissions of a certain thought-movement that looks maltreated in an alien language."

English, however, is not merely 'an alien language' to us ; it is, as Raja Rao himself adds, 'the language of our intellectual make up.' Whatever be the problems, some Indian writers in English have wielded it successfully, as would be evident from a careful perusal of the works by Raja Rao, Kamala Markandaya, G.V. Desani, Anita Desai, Arun Joshi, Salman Rushdie and others. As Krishna Kripalani maintains,

It is therefore hardly reasonable to belittle Indian writers who choose to write in English. In any case a writer has to be judged by the quality of his writing, irrespective of the medium he uses.[26]

The choice of a medium for self-expression is a matter of individual skill. The case of Joseph Conrad, born of Polish parents, is a good example of a writer who wrote his works in a language that was not his mother tongue and which he learnt at the age of nineteen, but was later honoured as a successful English writer. No individual or nation can today have any proprietorial claims over any language,[27] and a writer is free to express himself in any language provided he can do so successfully. Then, the English language found in some highly talented Indian writers' works has its own qualities, which have been noticed even by some perceptive Western critics. While reviewing Kamala Markandaya's *Possession*, Robert Payne, for example, points out the 'strange and beautiful' qualities of Indian English. He writes : "There is a lilt in it, and it seems inevitably to gather into a richness of colour and texture that is foreign to our more tepid skies. The important thing is that it is a language of its own, with its own history, its own way of looking at things."[28] It would be really interesting to see whether Indian novelists have succeeded in using English for their communicative purposes or not. If yes, what artifacts they have manipulated and in what way they have conveyed their thoughts and feelings without giving the impression of a sense of waste, If not, what prevented them from doing so.

The time has come when Indian writers have to forge an independent 'dialect' of English. Raja Rao wrote in his Foreword to *Kanthapura* : "We cannot write like the English. We should not. We can write only as Indians." What is absolutely essential is to evolve a distinctive medium of expression which would serve the purpose. "Our method of expression therefore," Raja Rao continues, "has to be a dialect which will some day prove to be as distinctive and colourful as the Irish or the American. Time alone will justify it." Indian English, however, has failed to emerge as a dialect ; at the most we have in it a few impressive idiolects. Joseph Furtado and Nissim Ezekiel, among poets, made sporadic efforts in this direction. But their efforts compare very unfavourably with those of, say, African poets. A well-known Indian poet himself admits that there is 'the absence of a linguistically respectable variety of Indian English'.[29] Most Indian writers' 'tongue' is 'in English chains' and they have to set it free at any cost. Gokak rightly suggests that Indian English has to represent "the evolution of a distinct standard —a standard the body of which is correct English usage, but whose soul is Indian in colour, thought and imagery."[30] One of the main problems before the Indian novelist writing in English is to evolve an Indian idiom, while conforming to the 'correctness' of English usage, which would help him express the unique quality of the Indian mind and sensibility.[31]

Besides the problem of English as a linguistic medium, the Indian novelist in English has to face many artistic problems, making sufficient allowance for the heterogeneous nature of his audience. These problems along with individual problems deserve thorough attention.[32] The earlier discussions of these issues have mostly generated more heat than light. The text-based analysis of the papers included in the present volume aims at thrashing the problems in a systematic manner.

Despite various problems and challenges, the Indian novel in English has proved its worth and potential. Its achievements can hardly be ignored, some of which have been enumerated earlier. The prose fiction in English by Indians has been found to be 'a meritorious outlet.'[33] It is undoubtedly "the most popular vehicle for the transmission of Indian ideas to the wider English-speaking world."[34] Indian fiction in English has a deeper significance than providing amusement. An intensive reading of it will give a clear idea of the cultural and social complex of India. That is why Dorothy Spencer regards Indian fiction in English as a major source for "a systematic study of cultural contact and cultural change, with Indian world view at the focus", which is most likely to increase the Western readers' "knowledge of acculturation process."[35] Any study of Indian fiction in English from the orientation of the Sociology of Literature will yield excellent results. This would be in addition to their value on purely artistic grounds. The rich harvest of talents in the Indian fiction in English has already enkindled the hope of still better productions. M.K. Naik has pertinently remarked :

... perhaps the best argument in support of the view that Indian writing in English is a body of works worth serious critical consideration is the fact that the best in it has been taken seriously and subjected to minute appraisal by critics in both India and abroad. ... The steady interest it has roused, in recent years, in English speaking countries shows that it has merits other than those of sheer novelty and exoticism.[36]

It's high time that the Indian fiction in English were studied from a comprehensive angle. The time has also come to evolve independent standards of evaluation free from the sedulous aping of the Western norms.

REFERENCES

1. K.R. Srinivasa Iyengar, "Indian Writing in English", in *Contemporary Indian Literature*, New Delhi : Sahitya Akademi, 1959, 2nd ed., p. 35.

2. Sir Jadunath Sarkar, *India Through the Ages*, Calcutta : S.C. Sarkar & Sons Ltd., 1944, p. 52.

3. G.B. Kanungo, *The Language Controversy in Indian Education* : Historical Study, Chicago : Comparative Education Center, 1962.

4. *The Miscellaneous Works of Thomas Babington Macaulay* ed. Lady Trevelyan, London; 1907, XIX, pp. 192-93.

5. Nirad C. Choudhuri, *The Continent of Circe*, Bombay : Jaico, 1966, p. 355.

6. William Walsh comments : "It was in 1930s that the Indians began what has now turned out to be their very substantial contribution to the novel in English and one peculiarly suited to their talents." "The Indian Sensibility in English," in C.D. Narasimhaiah (ed.), *Awakened Conscience*, New Delhi : Sterling Publishers, 1978, p. 66.

6 a. Meenakshi Mukherjee, *The Twice Born Fiction : Themes and Techniques of the Indian Novel in English*, New Delhi : Heinemann Educational Books, 1971, p. 22.

7. C. Paul Verghese, *Problems of the Indian Creative Writer in English*, Bombay : Somaiya Publications, 1971, pp. 124-125.

8. *A Study of Representative Indo-English Novelists*, New Delhi : Vikas Publishing House, 1976, pp. 1-6.

9. *Indian Writing in English*, Calcutta : Writers Workshop, 1964, p. 3.
10. *A Survey of Anglo-Indian Fiction*, London : OUP, 1934, pp. 309-10.
11. Atma Ram, *Interviews with Indo-English Writers*, Calcutta : Writers Workshop, 1983.
12. "Interview with Jasbir Jain", *Rajasthan University Studies in English*, 12 (1979), p. 5.
13. "Commonwealth Literature", *The Literary Criterion*, 14/3 (1979), p. 3.
14. K.R.S. Iyengar, "A General Survey", in Iqbal Bakhtiyar (ed.), *The Novel in Modern India*. The P.E.N. All India Centre, 1964.
15. "The Three Faces of an Indian", in Timothy O'Keefee (ed.), *Alienation*, London : McGibbon & Kee, 1960, pp. 80, 89. Elsewhere also Anant draws attention to Indians' 'dual code of behaviour' and 'moral inertia and flabbiness', which have forced them to be 'sucked into a shuffling, sleepwalking mass'. "The Hypnotized People", *Partisan Review*, 27/2 (1960), p. 312.
16. *The Intellectual Between Tradition and Modernity : The Indian Scene*. The Hague, 1961, p. 61.
17. S.C. Harrex, "A Sense of Identity : The Novels of Kamala Markandaya", *The Journal of Commonwealth Literature*, 6/1 (1971), p. 65.
18. For a detailed treatment, see R.S. Pathak, "The Indo-English Novelist's Quest for Identity", in R.K. Dhawan (ed.), *Explorations in Modern Indo-English Fiction*, New Delhi : Bahri Publications, 1982 and "What Ails the Indian Writer in English" ? *Journal of Literature and Aesthetics*, 3/1 (1983).
19. *Indo-Anglian Literature*, Bombay : International Book House, 1943, p. 29.
20. "Alienation and Identity", in Frank Johnson (ed.) *Alienation : Concept, Terms and Meaning*, New York, 1973, p. 84.
21. *Op. cit.*, p. 83.
22. "Literature of Protest", in Suresh Kohli (ed.), *Aspects of Indian Literature*, Delhi, 1975, p. 83.
23. M.D. Melwani, *Critical Essays on Indo-Anglian Themes*, Calcutta : Writers Workshop, 1971, p. 21.
24. *The Autobiography of an Unknown Indian* : London : Macmillan 1951, p. 262.
25. V.Y. Kantak, "The Language of Indian Fiction in English", in M.K. Naik *et al.* (eds.) *Critical Essays on Indian Writing in English*, Bombay : Macmillan Co. of India, 1977, p. 223.
26. *Literature of Modern India*, New Delhi : National Book Trust, 1985, p. 93.
27. K.R.S. Iyengar remarks : "English today is a shared language and no country—not even England—has any proprietorial rights over it." *Two Cheers for the Commonwealth*, Bombay ; Asia Publishing House, 1970, p. 24.
28. *The Saturday Review*, (23 May 1963), p. 34.

29.   R. Parthasarathy, [Introduction to *Ten Twentieth-Century Poets.* Delhi : OUP, 1967, pp. 3, 8.

30.   V.K. Gokak, *The Poetic Approach to Language,* London ; OUP, 1952, pp. 93-94.
      Even Balachandra Rajan, who is otherwise highly critical of Indian writing in English, talks of 'a continuing and vigorous interest in the creative possibilities' of Indian English.   See his article "India" in Bruce King (ed.), *Lite rature of the World in English,* London, 1974, p. 97.

31.   Cf. P. Lal ;   "I should like to add. . . that part of the excitement of writing in English [comes from the challenge of creating a special 'idiom'. . . .The task of any self-respecting Indian writer of English is to discover a suitable 'idiom' for the bewilderingly rich material he has in front of him waiting to be creatively transformed." C.D. Narasimhaiah (ed.), *Indian Literature of the Past Fifty Years, 1917-1967,* Mysore :   University of Mysore, 1970, pp. 34-35.

32.   Mukherjee, *op. cit.,* pp. 24, 13.   See also Verghese, *op. cit.*

33.   M.E. Derrett, *The Modern Indian Novel in English,* L'Institut de Sociologie, Universite Libre de Bruxelles, 1966, p. 8.

34.   H.M. Williams, *Indo-Anglian Literature, 1800-1990,* Orient Longman, 1976, p. 109.

35.   *Indian Fiction in English,* Philadelphia :   University of Pennsylvania Press, 1960, p. 11.

36.   "In Defence of Indian   Writing in English", in K.K. Sharma (ed.), *Indo-English Literature,* Ghaziabad :   Vimal Prakashan, 1977, p. 3.

1

Indian Fiction in English : Some Problems

R. C. SHUKLA

There has been an unprecedented efflorescence of Indian writing in English since independence. This is a rather queer phenomenon—queer in the sense that though we bade farewell to the English in 1947, the English language continues to be with us. All those of us who have had an English education cling to it like a small child clinging lovingly to the skirt of its foster mother. "One's own language is one's mother, but the language one adopts as a career, as a study, is one's wife and it is with one's wife that one sets up house", wrote Henry James to one of his French correspondents.[1] But I feel the metaphor of the foster-mother suits English better in the Indian context, And it is this metaphor that opens up a Pandora's box.

"An unfriendly spirit", writes V.Y. Kantak, "hovers all our creative writing in an alien tongue",[2] and English, though it may not be an exactly alien tongue for many of us, is, as Anita Desai aptly puts it, at best an immigrant in India :

> It is like a plant one would like to raise in one's garden —a beautiful but difficult one. One plants it in the sun—it doesn't do well. One pulls it out and plants it in the shade—it droops. One moves it to a damp spot— near fatal. Then to a dry one—equally bad. . . .It refuses to die but it never quite catches on either. It is a refugee in the land. Like a refugee it is astonishingly tenacious.[3]

Howsoever jubilant we may feel over the recognition accorded to Indian fiction in English by foreign critics like

Edmund Gosse, Graham Greene, William Walsh and others, it is still a fact that Indo-Anglian literature has not yet attained the sort of identity which American, Canadian and Australian literatures have done in their own contexts. The reason is not far to seek. Whereas English has taken roots —deep roots—in America, Canada and Australia, it has never taken roots in India. We continue to derive intellectual nourishment from it, but except in very few cases it has not been able to become the language of our emotional make up. The point has been very nicely brought out by Raja Rao in his foreward to *Kanthapura* :

> The telling [of the story] has not been easy. One has to convey in a language that is not one's own the spirit that is one's own. One has to convey the various shades and convolutions of certain thought movement that look maltreated in an alien language. I use the word 'Alien', yet English is not an alien language to us. It is the language of our intellectual make up like Sanskrit or Persian was before but not our emotional make up.[4]

There seems to be a constant tension between the native sensibility of the creative writer and the alien or acquired medium which he uses for the expression of this sensibility. Though sensibility is often treated as a universal faculty peculiar to mankind in general, yet we know that in its finer forms it is conditioned by a number of factors among which cultural heritage, social ethos, religious beliefs, family environment, heredity and education of the English language as the medium for expressing the typical Indian sensibility have been pointed out by a number of detractors of Indo-Anglian literature, who are still unwilling to believe that this literature has already flowered into a distinct type of creative writing in India with its own flavour and form. English is, undoubtedly, moulded to a different sensibility and demands uncommon skill on the part of the Indian writer to mould it to suit the Indian sensibility, which is very complex and invariably colours all our perceptions of reality, both consciously and unconsciously. It is not that the English language lacks adequacy. It is the richest language of the world and has also acquired a wonderful resilience under different types of pressures on account of its long association with various types of cultures. There is, however, a natural incompatibility between the English language and Indian sensibility and this incompatibility is much more glaring in the early Indian fiction in English, which was mostly experimental in nature, than in the later. The early Indian novelists in English turned out only poor imitations of the Victorian novelists. Their grasp over the language was uncertain and their choice of themes was guided by the works of the great contemporary writers in their native languages. B. Rajan Iyer's *Vasudev Sastri* (1905), A. Madhavaiah's *Thillai Govindan* (1912) Jogendera Singh's *Nasreen* (1915), Balkrishna's *The Love of Kusuma* (1910), for example, are all very feeble as works of literature. The language is redolent of native verbosity and inordinate love of similes and metaphors. Here is a passage from *Vasudev Sastri* ;

> He was. . . .a middle-aged man of fair-complexion and well proportioned limbs ; his face had a calmness and serenity in it, a gentleness, a sweetness and luxuriant cheerfulness like that of a full blown lotus which an ancient *rishi* might have envied : and in his large, beautiful eyes, there was an angelic expression of goodness, which by its silent and magic could have soothed the anger of a Durvasa.[5]

The later writers have, however, succeeded, to a great extent, in getting over this incompatibility. They have also been helped by the fact that our long association with English along with our westernised education and the prolonged East-West contacts have atleast partly modified our sensibility and set it in better tune with the English language as medium of expression.

Many of the later Indo-Anglian writers have had their education in England and have lived there for long periods assiduously immersing themselves in western intellectual traditions. This has helped them in looking at Indian life and traditions objectively and in imbibing the ability to handle the English language in a more effective manner.

But even in these cases, the gain has not been an unmixed one. They have developed either a split sensibility or an inordinate love for verbal brilliance. A comparison of R.K. Narayan with B. Rajan will illustrate the point. Both of them have written novels based on life in South India but there is a vast difference in their language and style. Here is a passage from *The Guide* :

> I awaited the receipt of certain data before venturing to answer. The data was how much time and money he was going to spend, Malgudi and its surroundings were my special show. I could let the man have a peep at it or a whole panorama. It was *adjustible*, I could give them a glimpse of a few hours or soak them in mountain or river scenery or archeology for a whole week. I could not really decide how much to give or withhold until I knew how much cash the man carried or if he carried a chequebook, how good it was.[6]

Narayan is telling us in it about an ordinary character—a guide, whose main aim is to get the maximum from the tourists. His narration is straight-forward and realistic. It has an undercurrent of irony. The language is simple and unobtrusive. It is, however, perfectly in tune with the tenor of the story-telling. There is practically no tension between the matter and the medium of the story teller.

Now let us take a passage from B. Rajan's *The Dark Dancer* (1959). Describing the beginning of the trauma of the partition of the country, the writer remarks :

> The Award was the match that lit the long train of dynamite, snaking and ravaging across the chosen frontier. The violence broke out of honourable men, a lust in their eyes, a smear of satisfaction on the thirsting knives, the burning home its beacon and memorial. The words, the inflamed reports, the provocative rumours, were like bacteria in the air that one breathed and before reason could summon its reserves against the menace, the contagion had seized you and you were its screaming puppet.[7]

As compared to Narayan, Rajan has greater verbal brilliance, poeticisms and literary flourish. His vocabulary is obviously richer and he has the desire to make a show of it. Naturally, the language overshoots the demands of the narrative. The style is obviously verbose and dilutes the intensity of even the most moving experience. Any brilliant passage from *The Dark Dancer* invariably illustrates that the novelist's academic absorption rarely allows him to be natural. Narayan's vocabulary may be limited and like Addison's his sentences may rarely burst into brilliance, but he knows the art of moulding his medium according to the needs of his sensibility and experience.

Raja Rao, too, has shown uncommon skill in handling the English language in spite of his preoccupation with abstruse metaphysics, but this is more true of his language and style in *Kanthapura* than *The Serpent and the Rope*. In the later novel his English seems to be creaking and cracking under the load of Sanskrit vocabulary and Kannad sentence patterns. Seasoning the English vocabulary with native words or phrases has been a common device to naturalise it but Raja Rao has probably overdone the trick in his 'philosophical' novel to mitigate the abstruseness of his theme with local colour.

The post - independence writers have learnt a lot from their senior colleagues and handle the English language almost as naturally as it can be possible for a creative writer who knows it only as an adopted medium of expression. They seem to have moved a long way from the literally—translated vocabulary of Punjabi bawdry of early Mulk Raj Anand or the faltering, hesitant, short sentences of the early short-story writer R. K. Narayan. It has now become obvious that Indianness cannot be superimposed on English. The creative writer must learn to use it naturally without forcing too many native words on it or dislocating drastically its characteristic syntax. He must recreate it as a suitable medium for expressing his sensibility. Some younger Indo-Anglian writers like G.V. Desani, Anita Desai and Kamala Markandaya have made this sort of creative use of the English language.

The second problem is that of themes. There has been no dearth of themes for the Indian fiction writers in English. But this almost infinite variety itself has presented many pitfalls along their way to enduring success. They have till now tried their hands on themes ranging from the purely Indian to the purely exotic. Old legends, myths, history, social evils, the struggle for freedom, the traumatic experience of partition, the tragic dilemma of East-West encounter, the alienation caused by the breaking up of the joint family system, the ever-increasing exodus of the rural folk to the urban industrial areas, the onslaught of the materialistic western culture and the resultant snapping of the closely knit old human ties and the fast erosion of old values and beliefs—all have been handled in a more or less experimental way by Indian novelists in English. Quite a few of them have tried to dole out various shades of Indian philosophy and spiritual beliefs in the garb of very thinly woven tales. It is only recently that themes of alienation, rootlessness and emotional or spiritual vacuity have been taken up to catch up with the fast-moving fiction in the West. Faint undertones of surrealism and existentialism are also discernible in a few cases.

Choosing the right theme is not difficult when the writer picks it up from the solid ground of his own life-experience in the midst of the widest possible segment of humanity. Difficulties crop up when the writer concentrates on the too narrow personal experiences in a close circle or tries to weave a story around a theme chosen by him on account of some academic or emotional predilection. The main difficulty with the Indian fiction writer in English is that he is generally cut off from the masses and seldom draws the material for his creative writing from the lives of the vast majority of common people, as Mulk Raj Anand or R.K. Narayana did. Many of them have easily succumbed to the treacherous lure of contemporary or historical themes of purely journalistic interest or the much more disastrous temptation of imitating the academically acclaimed contemporary foreign writers.

Let us first consider the novels that have a social theme. The Indianness of the Indian writer of fiction in English is best reflected in the novels on social themes, because in these cases the writers are easily able to connect themselves with the most glorious tradition of Indian novels. The concentration on social themes often precludes eccentricity and freakish originality. The dialectical relationship between the individual and society is of perennial interest and can be explored on various levels. The multiplicity of these levels provides scope for originality and depth. J.D. Brunton writes :

> India had many of the cultural conditions favourable to the novel before she came into contact with Europe. But now she has social forces actively favourable to the production of fiction : a large audience, an educated class, a new questioning of ageold socio-religious dogma and a consuming urge for knowledge and interpretation of society. Henry James's complaint about the difficulties for the practicising novelist inherent in the amorphous monotony of American society is well known. The Indian novelist has, instead, an extraordinary cultural multiplicity to contemplate, embracing differences of age, caste: religion, wealth and politics.[8]

It is strange that novelists should ignore this vast field of surging life and retire into the narrow cell of the self as if it stood by itself. The analysis of the self in complete isolation from society is a projection into literature of the growing individualism fostered by decadent western culture in its search for psychological solace, without reforming itself. It is ever-expanding human relationship that lends new dimensions to the self and makes its ordeals dramatic and significant.

Stunned by the success of the Indian godmen in the west, many indo-Anglian writers are tempted to give a spiritualistic window-dressing to their themes, without realizing that religion, philosophy and spirituality are extremely amorphous, nebulous and complex in the Indian context. Aldous Huxley felt that spirituality "is the primal curse of India and the cause of all her misfortunes."[9]

It will be wrong to suggest that the only concern of a vast number of Indians is, and has always been, the realisation of the spirit. This view could be maintained only by ignoring a great part of the cultural heritage of India. "Indian history does not consist merely of the Buddhas and Sankaras. There were Kautilyas and Vatsyayans as well. The down-to-earth wisdom of the *Panchatantra*, the economic and social oppression of the majority by a minority, the gross eroticism in much of Indian art and literature—these are not quite equal to the exalted 'spirituality' claimed."[10]

Moreover, it is only for exceptionally great philosophers to disentangle the highly entangled strands of religion, philosophy and superstition and novelists are not philosophers in the academic sense. In spite of many accolades, most of the philosophy in *The Serpents and the Rope* has failed to be an integral part of the novel. It has only added profundity to the confusion engendered by the purely imaginary and artificially stage-managed encounters of East and West through the unhappy marriage of the South Indian Brahmin boy Ram and the French girl Madeleine. Passages like the following do not add anything to the reader's knowledge of the self or the world :

> Unless the masculine principle absorbs the feminine, the world cannot be annihilated, and so there can be no joy. Joy is not in the thought, but as it were in the thought of the thought in *'ma pense'e s'est pense'e'* of Mallarme'. In fact, it is only in the stuff of thought, that is, where there is no thought.

Serious-minded literary critics have not liked the overdose of philosophy in the novel. Brunton comments : "So much blurring and vagueness of definition can only stem from uncertainty on the part of the author; and this weakness, in the work of such a patently intelligent writer, must in turn be largely due to the hunt for that vague chimera, the 'Indian Novel'. The repetitions of Benares, Himalaya and Ganges, Siva and Parvati, tiger and cobra are too insistent not to be conscious fabrications, the wistful symbols of the novelist striving to discover Indianness".[11]

The quality of Indianness is not to be imposed on any creative form of writing from outside; it must be inherent in the sensibility of the writer. He must be fully and genuinely aware of his Indianness, without isolating himself from the traditions of the West. Unfortunately, most of the Indo-Anglian writers lack this awareness both on the emotional and spiritual levels. They belong to a small group that has grafted itself on to the Western way of life and thinking and have, thus, become victims of emotional rootlessness.

There has been, however, great improvement in the attitude of the younger writers and they have been writing successfully as Indians who are also aware of the human predicament in the West. The impartial sensitiveness and preception with which the post-independence celebrities of Indian fiction in English have written about partition and the other cataclysmic development in the country and in the souls of men and women, deserve all praise.

III

I shall close this paper with a brief discussion of the most disturbing of all the problems—for whom does the Indian novelist in English write ? Does he write for his own countrymen or just for those foreigners who are interested in India ? The number of English-knowing people in India has been constantly on the increase. Though the majority of these people live in towns and cities and form a sort of elitist group, yet they are not isolated from the common people like the elite of the pre-independence days. These people who are keenly interested in all that is written by their countrymen in English, are, in truth, the best judges and real patrons of Indo-Anglian writing, howsoever large may be the sale of this writing outside India. And though every now and then a Booker Award or the Reader's Best Selection and various other prizes instituted in England and America may be bagged by these writers, their best prize shall always be their acceptance by the vast majority of their Indian readers. Whenever their works have true merit, international recognition will come to them in natural course. They cannot win this just by picking up foreign characters and events and jostling them with the native ones. Most of the foreign characters created by them lack credibility and genuine spark of life. It is hightime that we learnt that we can go out on to the vast ocean of surging humanity all over the world by first learning to swim in the national stream. There has been, till now, little effort to acquaint the readers of fiction in Indian languages with the achievements of Indian fiction in English. A concerted attempt in this direction can be made by translating the best of Indian fiction in English into major Indian languages. Such an attempt will help the Indo-Anglian writing in becoming an integral part of the great creative venture on the national level.

REFERENCES

1. Quoted in Anita Desai. "The Indian Writer's Problems"; in *Explorations in Modern Indo-English Fiction*, edited by R.K. Dhawan, p. 235.
2. "The language of Indian Fiction in English", in *Critical Essays on Indian Writing in English*, edited by M.K. Naik, S.K. Desai and G.S. Amur, p 223.
3. *Ibid*, p. 224.
4. Foreword to *Kanthapura*.
5. "Vasudev Sastri", in B. Rajan Iyer's *Rambles in Vedanta*, Madras, 1905.
6. R.K. Narayan, *The Guide*, p. 54.
7. B. Rajan, *The Dark Dancer*, 1959.
8. J.D. Brunton, "India in Fiction", in *Critical Essays on Indian Writing in English*, p. 214.
9. Aldous Huxley, *Jesting Pilate*, p. 109.
10. *India : Myth and Reality*, p. 3.
11. *Critical Essays on Indian Writing in English*, p. 215.

2

Existentialism in Anand's Across the Black Waters

S. C. DWIVEDI

Across the Black Waters shows a close resemblance to what is known as existentialist art. It throws light on existential concepts such as meaninglessness, alienation and subjectivity through the powerful characterization of its several characters including its hero, Lalu Singh. The novel tells us about the limitation of the human life and "the mystery of existence, infinitude and guilt, death and hope, freedom and meaning". Lalu Singh, the hero of the novel, is "transcendent by virtue of his nakedness rather than his communal authority". He searches for self-definition and freedom and ultimately retreats into self-hood.

The pattern of experience in *Across the Black Waters* is largely existential as it is composed of contradiction, chance, illusory choice, horrors of war, absurdity and nothingness. Lalu Singh observes that his condition is shaped by fear and loneliness and there is endless suffering in his existence. Again and again he demonstrates his appetite to comprehend the absolute and the need to unite things to his own self and finds the utter impossibility of reducing this world to a rational and logical order. There are no resolutions of the mental conflicts, agonies and turmoils raging in Lalu Singh's soul. He is confronted with the problem of understanding things in human terms and the more he tries the more he fails. Thus the novel dramatizes

the process by which Lalu Singh's illusions about a rational
order are destroyed and brings it to a point of climax
when Lalu Singh finds himself cut off from his authentic
existence. His experiences as a soldier in the battlefield of
France in World War I, when Indian troops land in Marcilles, make him a stranger in the face of the absurdities of
war and consequent turmoils, agonies, indifference, tiredness
and depression. The tremor of dread speads like a panic in
his brain and the confusion of silence and horrors of war
overpower him completely. While the oppressions of war
render him completely unable to relate outside his own self,
his inner urges, struggles, hopes, aspirations as an Indian
soldier in France indicate alienation from the self. Anand
is not an existentialist like Sartre, Kafka, Camus, John
Macquarie, but his passionate desire to go deep into the
dilemmas of existence, suffering, alienation and fear bring
him closer to them.

Anand's *Across the Black Waters* is an example of universal aspect of human experience. The novel may be
studied as an existentialist critique, since it rejects the
ready-made myth or symbol. Lalu Singh's commitment is
existentialist as it is born of the desire to express the independence of his self in a world without meaning. Although
his is not the only quest in the novel, it has the truth of his
subjective experience. Lalu Singh is committed to his quest
with passionate experience. Anand describes the battlefields of France in World War I and the inner struggles of
the Indian troops in Marcilles from an existentialist angle.
He deals with the concept of freedom which corresponds to
his own vision of life and human responsibility. He is
greatly worried about the loss of human dignity and degradation of human values. The novel had its origin in Anand's
attempt to resolve the dilemma of the individual *versus*
society, the mind *versus* matter. The novelist describes the
primitive and universal aspect of human experience. He
here adores the uniqueness and subjectivity of person and
rejects ready-made ideologies. He emphasizes what is
lived instead of what is thought about fighting and warfare.

Anand describes in *Across the Black Waters* the felt experiences of his characters in order to know their subjectivity, despair, crisis, dread, choice, commitment, freedom, transcendence, authenticity, and humanism. He dwells on nature of pain and loneliness as central to human existence, the subjectivity and idiosyncracies of the characters. Anand wants us to understand the fundamental existentialist truth : existence precedes essence. Lalu Singh and other characters first exist as human beings and define themselves only later in relation to war. The novelist raises questions which can be properly understood in terms of existentialist thought. An analysis of the novel shows Anand's preference for human life and the nature of man, his increasing concern, his loneliness and his attempt to come to grips with himself.

Across the Black Waters is set in the battlefield of France of the period of World War I, when Indian troops landed in Marcilles, made their way by train or road and got engaged in neck-to-neck fighting with the Germans. It deals with the period when the British Raj was at its zenith and the British rulers were held in high esteem. The writer recreates the atmosphere of war with great authenticity. As G.S. Balram Gupta observes, "Not only was his father a regular soldier, but Anand also is by no means a stranger to wars, since he has close glimpses of the two giant wars fought in his generation. Naturally, his descriptions of the various phases of war and the hazardous life of the soldiers ring perfectly true." In this novel Anand has recreated all the horrors and brutality of war. The novelist has depicted the inner urges, struggles, hopes and aspirations of the Indian soldiers in those times. Anand says," This book was sketched out in a rough draft in Barcelona, Madrid during January and April 1937, and entirely written in Chinnor, Oxon, between July and December 1939." Anand loves to portray the realistic pictures of life of soldiers and aims at demolishing and exposing the imperialism of war. The Indian soldiers considered the war as devoid of all meaning. Anand has aptly described their attitude to war in the following passage :

Where was the war ? How was it being fought and what would the sepoys be asked to do ? The questions flashed through his eager mind. But there was no answer. And there was a dread about the future he sought to drown this train of thought in a melody... The thought seemed to return, however. If only there was not this discreet veil of silence drawn over the movement of the troops of the Sarkar which everything to rumours and legends.

This appropriately demonstrates the existentialist condition of Lalu Singh. The Sarkar further aggravated this condition by not disclosing various facts of the new and its objective. Everything was left to rumour and legends, and these increased the indefiniteness and alienation of the sepoys. Lalu Singh looks before and after in this novel and pines for what he does not get ; even his hopes, joys and laughters are mixed with a certain amount of pain and loneliness and more often than not we like this novel because of his fragments of confession and existentialist statements. He does not know that his life like his colleagues' is completely shallow, that they live like strangers in the world. The Sarkar and its war have rendered them into a cog in a machine and they no longer experience life in its totality. The soldiers naturally long for fellowship and authenticity. The novelist says :

Some stood by sacks and rifles and others sat on collections of kitbags, apparently waiting for orders. Everywhere there was the wild confusion of loud talk and furious gesticulation; the rustling of clothes, the movement of forms. But there was a glow of warmth among the sepoys, a strange sense of fellowship, as if they felt they ought to hang together because they were going farther into the unknown.

The alienated soldiers form a community among themselves, the kind of community that aloneness creates, Lalu Singh's dread uniting him with the dread of other soldiers. Since everybody's future is uncertain, indefinite and shrouded in mystery, they cling to each other with a strange sense of fellowship. That is the existential thing which the novel aims to delienate. These characters already alone and hard beset make a brave choice. Their resolve that "they ought to hang together because they were going farther into the unknown" is an existential decision. These characters show that man cannot live without freedom and choice. It is through freedom and choice that Lalu Singh adjusts himself in the battlefield. Lalu Singh and his friends are shown in actual action. As M.K. Naik points out, "it would be unfair to describe *Across the Black Waters* as only a war novel". Whereas the novel paints an authentic picture of war, it is actually a complex mosaic of several other themes which recur in Anand's works—themes such as the contrast between the Indian tradition and Western Modernity, the relationship between Indians and white men and the exploitation of the lowly by those in power and authority. The facination of the novel lies not in its being either a war novel or depicting Indian and Western tradition. What Naik fails to notice is that all human beings—Indian, Western, traditional or modern seek freedom and choice in their own way. Man cannot get rid of freedom and choice. As Sartre observes, "In one sense choice is possible, but what is not possible is not to choose, but I must know that if I do not choose, that is still a choice." Though Naik uses the word 'authentic' he does so in relation to war and forgets the human beings whose existence is much more authentic and it is their authenticity which endows them with a sense of universality in the novel. Take the example of Lalu Singh. He chooses to express and when he does so he does not speak for himself but also for mankind in general. Choice is the essential part of Lalu's existence with which he cannot part. This is how Lalu Singh describes the utter absurdity and meaninglessness of war :

> He [Lalu Singh] could not belive that ordinary men and women of good sense, and the Government of France, England and Germany, which were saner and wiser than the ordinary people over whom they ruled, could be engaged in a war in which men were being wounded and houses shattered.

There is in this passage more than the mere description of the destructive power of war. Lalu Singh instinctively decries and derigrades war and also the governments of France, England, and Germany which indulge in war. Here he speaks like a sage, a Rishi, who is both a seer and a speaker. He ponders over the futility and inauthenticity of war because then and then alone he can arrive at his own authenticity. It is his authenticity, freedom and choice that matter more in the novel than all the descriptions of war. Existentially it is the war seen through the eyes of Lalu Singh, felt and experienced by him that is important to any reader of the novel. Lalu Singh's choice is not for himself but for mankind in general. The novel deals with his growth as an existentialist hero. Lalu Singh is a wandering Indian peasant, later a soldier of the first world war, and lastly a leader of the peasant movement.

In *Across the Black Waters* Anand condemns nihilism and propagates peace. The characters of this novel have been drawn from the world of labour. It is quite natural that they aspire for peace and happiness The novelist presents before us the life of trenches. The Indian soldiers have joined English Army not because they have any love for the Government or the war but because they cannot tolerate the pangs of hunger and poverty. They experience the horror of war every moment and live in dread and fear. The following passage of the novel clearly demonstrates Lalu Singh's passion for peace and freedom. The horror of war has not only curtailed his freedom but completely annihilated it and he observes meaninglessness and absurdity everywhere :

> He [Lalu Singh] gazed at Mars, the star of war, which he had come to recognise on the voyage from its readers but apart from its brilliance there seemed no meaning in it.

Lalu Singh speaks here as a person who has been denied his individuality, authenticity and subjectivity. What he surveys in the above lines is nothing but meaninglessness and alienation. The above words describe the deflation of the blood-red Mars which symbolises the absurdity of the death of the Indian soldiers who have been alienated from their native land and driven across the "black waters" in foreign countries to die in the selfish name of the imperia-

lists. All the soldiers participating in war feel the irrationa-
lity of war and express this feeling powerfully. It is their
actions, thoughts, hopes, fears, dread, anguish, and alienation and their search for freedom and retreat into selfhood
which are of universal interest to us.

There prevails deep dissatisfaction among the soldiers
regarding war. Anand tells us about the impact of war
which meant nothing but a holocaust of men, beasts and
houses. The soldiers wondered why it was being fought at
all. The majority of soldiers got out of hand. They refused
to follow blindly the plans of monopolists who were their
real enemies. The soldiers are deeply interested in their
selfhood and inwardness. They cannot go against their
inwardness and subjectivity which are much more valuable
to them than the blind plans of the monopolists. Mutual
understanding and a warm sense of fellowship—a type of
fellowship that aloneness and strangeness often create-
contribute to the awakening of their inwardness. Anand
has drawn memorable scenes of their inwardness. The
following passage throws ample light on the inwardness of
Lalu Singh :

> Instead of laughing or smiling as the others did, Lalu
> found himself contracting into his own skin, till he felt
> himself reduced to an emptiness from the centre of
> which his two eyes seemed to see this world as an enor-
> mous enclosure, crowded by hordes of hard, gigantic
> shapes which were oppressing him. In order not to sit
> aside, apart from his companions, he tried to persuade
> himself that he was happy, as happy as Subah and
> Baluchi. And he tried to put on a smile and thought
> of saying something. But his eyes met Subah's and the
> deliberate smile on his face broke up into the edges of a
> nervous laugh which suddenly stopped short and gave
> place to a grim, set expression.

The helpless Lalu is pitted against the horrors of war. In
the above lines we notice how his contraction, emptiness,
oppression, anguish, dread and the deliberate smile on his
face breaking up into a nervous laugh convey his existential
condition. For the poor Lalu, victory of existence lies in
the process of defeat not in the smile but in anguish, and
he retreats into his selfhood like a true existentialist hero.

Lalu's contracting into his own skin, pervading emptiness and his nervousness only emphasize his subjectivity. Here, Anand stresses Lalu's concrete existence, his search for freedom and his consequent responsibility for what he does and makes himself to be.

Anand is always interested in depicting the personal real of the individual from beginning to end. He treats the existentialist frame of reference as the individual's own frame of reference in meeting reality. He powerfully presents individual fears, hopes and the actions, movements and rhythms of living persons confronting the world with all their strength. Anand's own assertion as a novelist comes quite close to that of the existentialists :

> All these heroes, as the other men and women who had in my novels and short stories, were dear to me, because they were reflections of the real people I had known during my childhood and youth. And I was only repaying the debt of gratitude I owe them for much of my inspiration they had given me to mature into manhood. When I began to interpret their lives in my writing. They were not mere phantoms ... They were flesh of my flesh and blood of my blood, and obsessed me in the way in which certain human beings obsess an artist's soul. And I was doing no more than what a writer does when he seeks to interpret the truth from the realities of his life.

As it is clear from Anand's own words, he is immensely interested in the flesh and blood of his characters which were in a way the flesh and the blood of the novelist himself. He is talking of their contingent nature, subjectivity, inwardness of his characters like an existentialist artist. Through the subjectivity the characters of this novel choose and make of themselves. This novel is very different from what Anand has written earlier. The novel is set in the battlefields of France, the theme that completely baffles the Indian sepoys since they find themselves surrounded by an unending darkness. The bewilderment of the sepoys regarding war is aptly described :

> Where was the war ? How was it being fought and what would the sepoys be asked to do. The questions flashed through his eager mind, but there was no answer. As there was a dread about the future he sought

to drown the train of thoughts in a melody. ... The thought seemed to return, however. If only there was not this discreet veil of silence drawn over the movements of troops by the Sarkar which left everything to rumours and legends.

Lalu spoke this when he was going to the station on the mule carts. There was not much time at his disposal for idle reflection as the mule carts were almost ready to proceed and the contingent with which Lalu had to go to the station was ready. As he rode away, he pondered deeply over the subject of war. The more he thought about it the more he was confused. He saw utter futility in participating in it. Lalu saw the human freedom and dignity threatened to an unusual degree and the existence of the human person as a whole in danger. He found himself in a world shattering situation. He found things falling apart before his eyes. Lalu's utterance, "And there was a dread about future he sought to drown the train of thoughts in a melody"—points towards his existential condition. The passage throws ample light on Lalu's deep-sense of dread which is a strong existential category. His dread is created out of the uncertainity about the future. These questions haunt his mind all the time—Where was the war? Why was it being fought ? What good will it bring to the Indian sepoy ? But he does not find satisfactory answer and encounters dread and despair instead. This consciousness of incapacity to express his freedom fills in him the feelings of dread, fear, anguish and insecurity. The Sarkar has left everything to "rumours and legends" and the sepoys feel much wounded and frustrated because of this. As they reach the station, they see the turmoil and confusion all around. Anand gives its description in these words :

As they got to the station the scene was one of complete turmoil. Some of the sepoys on fatigue duty were hauling things into the supply wagons, shouting and swearing as they strained to lift the weights, and being shouted and sworn at by the N C.O's. Some stood by the stacks and rifles and others sat on collection of kitbags, apparently waiting for orders. Everywhere there

was the wild confusion of loud talk and furious gesticulation, the rustling of clothes, the movement of forms.
But there was a glow of warmth among the sepoys, a
strange sense of fellowship, as if they felt that they
ought to hang together because they were going farther
into the unknown. He felt he was nothing about them.

The use of words like 'turmoil', 'fatigue' 'unknown'
'wild confusion' in the above passage only signals the
existential condition of the soldiers. With the help of these
words the novelist gives the definition of their lives in order
to deal with experience. The soldiers suffer from insecurity,
crisis and indefiniteness. This is also the existentialist fate
of all humanity which is adequately explained by the novelist in this novel, Lalu is a typical existentialist hero around
whom the whole novel moves. We are attracted by his
authentic existence and begin to see the war and people
participating in it as Lalu sees them. Though Anand primarily wrote it as a war novel with his preconceived Mar-
xist notions, the posterity may like to read it as a novel of
human predicament where the interest may not be so much
dry and drab reality as the problematic relation between
individual behaviour and social function with an emphasis
on the "felt life" of Henry James or the "lived" experiences
of F.R. Leavis.

Thus, Lalu Singh moves within a framework that is existentialist. It is he who narrates the novel and he chooses
to express rightly. The meaning of war almost unsettles his
mind and we find him disturbed in arguing for the validity
of his search for the truth about the existence. His commitment is existentialist as it is born of the desire to express
the freedom of his self in a world that to him has lost
meaningful significance. Though his quest is not the only
quest in the novel, it has the validity of subjective experience. The remarkable point is that Lalu is committed to
his quest with passionate sincerity. Since his quest is not
false, he shows a very high degree of consciousness of
one's self-indeed. The story, as it is told by Lalu, unfolds
the journey of the human soul. Lalu's participation in war
endows him with the opportunity to encounter with his

existence and its mysteries. Lalu lives with his doubts, dread, despair and alienation and exercises his choice to express freedom constantly. He unfailingly chooses a way of action and a way of belief which is peculiarly his own. Investigation into the self (*atmanam viddhi*) is the proclamation of the Upanishads also. The novel is full of Lalu's investigations into the self. It tells about his inward journey and imminent tensions. As Lalu says in the novel while stating his thoughts about war and its impact on sepoys, "The air and water of this place is different. And because we were separated and put with English and French regiments, most of the sepoys felt that no one knew anything about us, and some of the sepoys not knowing the language, lost their way ... and it was...like hell". This is the type of inner ascent that almost every page of the novel offers to its readers. Not only the character of Lalu but the whole pattern of existence as revealed in the novel is largely existentialist, as it is composed of alienation, subjectivity, freedom, and choice. *Across the Black Waters* is an existentialist novel where the characters discover and rediscover their world exclusively in terms of themselves. Anand offers the existentialist aspect of man as the universal view of man. Existentialism in this novel should be taken as a means of transcending the limiting conditions of war and society.

Across the Black Waters is a significant existentialist novel in so far as it tells about the fierce, hostile and indifferent atmosphere of the Great War and conveys the tragic death of Kirpu, Dhanno, and Lachaman. Lalu Singh loves life irrepressibly despite all odds and his keen desire to live makes this novel existentialist in the true sense of the term. This is how Anand has described Lalu's condition in the end of the novel :

He wanted to live and he tried to buoy himself up by refusing to contemplate his own doom. But the thought of the possibility that he might be finished returned. His eyes caught the gleam of the bayonet on his rifle and he shrank at the thought of being degutted. Now that he had looked one possibility in the face, another stared at him ; he might be shot in some limb which might disable him or disfigure him. Still that would be better than utter extinction. But no woman would even at look at him. He could not bear the humiliation. He had rather go clean out of life. But he might be saved. He wanted to believe that he would be So he sensored his thoughts and listened to the barrage.

Lalu Singh wants to live or die like a true human being and discovers in the process that human survival is suicidal and knowing life is really knowing death. It is the continual and violent refreshing of the idea of discovery of the self that he seeks his existentialist freedom. He is continually defining the reality of his individual consciousness against the fierce atmosphere of war. He, therefore, wishes to go clean out of life. The novel departs from abstract philosophical theories towards the search for philosophical insights based on the lives of the human beings whom Anand knew in flesh and blood. The characters of the novel reveal a great urge to express themselves at all costs so as to expose the abstract humanity with a view to deliberately dramatizing the passions of concrete humanity. *Across the Black Waters* contains concrete pictures of the disturbed, nervous, and paranoaic consciousness of the people like Kirpu, Lalu, Subah, Lok Nath, Owen Sahib and others.

In sum, *Across the Black Waters* is a powerful existentialist novel which should be read as an authentic account of the thoughts and actions of Lalu Singh and his other colleagues participating in the war. It is concerned with the development of Lalu Singh's thought as well as growth of his personality. His actions as well as perceptions are involved and we are drawn to them as we read the novel. Loneliness and strange sense of fellowship are the twin modes of Lalu Singh's authentic existence, for which *Across the Black Waters* is a brilliant metaphor. While one would not say that Anand is an existentialist, he is not incompatible with the existentialist position. In so far as *Across the Black Waters* repudiates the adequacy of any political, social, military or cultural body of belief and expresses marked dissatisfaction with traditional philosophy and systems as superficial, banal and irrelevant through its hero Lalu Singh and other characters, it demonstrates the importance of existence and life over essence and theory.

REFERENCES

1. Mulk Raj Anand, *Across the Black Waters* (Orient Paperbacks, 1980). All textual references are to this edition.
2. G.S. Balram Gupta, *Mulk Raj Anand* (Bareilly : Prakash Book Depot., 1974), pp. 58-63.
3. M.K. Naik, *Mulk Raj Anand* (London : Arnold-Heinemann, 1973), pp. 62-70.
4. M.N. Sinha, *A Primer of Existentialism* (Delhi : Capital Publishing House, 1982), p. 68.
5. M.K. Naik, S.K. Desai and G.S. Amur (eds.), *Critical Essays on Indian Writing in English* (Dharwar : Karnatak University, 1968), pp. 16-30.
6. K.N. Sinha (ed.), *Indian Writing In English* (New Delhi : Heritage, 1979), pp. 1-18.
7. Ruby Chatterji (ed.), *Existentialism in American Literature* (Delhi : Arnold Heinemann, 1983), pp. 17-30.

3

An Endless Search :
A Psychoanalytical Study of Ananta
in Mulk Raj Anand's 'The Big Heart'

H.S.S. BAIS

Though much has been written about Mulk Raj Anand's main themes and technique by Marlen Fisher, Saros Cowasjee, Alastair Niven, K.K. Sharma, G.S. Balram Gupta, M.K. Naik, Margaret Berry, Jack Lindsey, D. Riemenschneider, K.N. Sinha, K.R. Srinivas Iyengar and others, it seems to me that this voluminous critical appraisal of Anand is only the one eighth of the iceberg of his art. The real Anand and his art still appears to be ellusive. What K.K. Sharma has hinted at is a suggestion to critics to concentrate more on the part hidden under the sea of Anand's overwhelming themes. He remarks :

> Anand also distinguishes between the modern novel and the novel written in earlier times. According to him, while the novel in the previous centuries was obviously concerned with moral values, the modern novel lays stress on the individual's psychological life and motivations.[1]

It seems that the real motive of writing the novels like *The Coolie, The Untouchable* and *The Big Heart*, was not so much to prop the economical or social questions of the Indian Society during a period which was the most crucial in many ways, but to unravel the meaning and purpose of creative writing. What is not obvious is the declaration by

Anand in many of his letters, interviews, talks and non-fictional writings, which convey Anand's philosophy of creative writing, as to what actually he wanted to say through the characters of his novels.

In "A Novel Form in the Ocean of Story", he says :

This concept of 'Karuna' or Compassion came to men and women in travail as the first inunciation of expiation through art, centuries before Aristotle's famous 'Catharsis'.[2]

According to Anand, 'Karuna' being the essential ingredient in the creation of literature, the writer cannot but remain untouched deeply. There has to be a very close relationship between the writer and the element of compassion. After all, the thing which a writer tries to convey must have meant a great deal to him ; otherwise he would have lived without ever having expressed his ideas about it. Anand further remarks :

We might have been able to extend our own consciousness as also to invoke 'Karuna' from which alone any literature can be justified. ...I can tell you that what is significant in our time is the assertion of love for human beings, specially in their own weaknesses, in their dignity of their frailty, and in the utter wretchedness.[3]

Iyengar traces the influence of Anand's mother on him and says that the personality of the mother had many effects on the thinking of Anand. He observes : "From his peasant mother he doubtless derived his commonsense, his sense of the ache at the heart of Indian Humanity, and his understanding compassion for the waifs, the disinherited, the lowly, the last—Daridra Narayan."[4]

Thus, it becomes necessary to keep oneself a little away from the trend of evaluation done so far, to have a deeper understanding of the art of Mulk Raj Anand. His art of fiction writing would be found to be multidimensional if the characters' minds are probed deeply. On the surface level, they seem to be strongly motivated by the search for finding a way out of the quagmire of the most basic needs like food, shelter and sex. But within them a fire burns continuously. This fire is of the great quest for finding solutions to the questions of identity, freedom, adjustment between tradition and modernity, morality of action and thought, individuality and community, the complexity of politicization of all human endeavour and death and im- mortality. Before all these questions are dealt with, let us have a look at the basic concept and structure of the novel *The Big Heart.*

Ananta, a coppersmith, returns to his home-town of Amritsar after having worked in Bombay and Ahmedabad. He brings with him Janki, a young widow, whom he loves and who is now slowly dying of tuberculosis. In Amritsar, Ananta resumes his hereditory trade, but like most people of his brotherhood he has difficulty in making a living. The introduction of machines has thrown the artisans out of work. Though Ananta suffers because of the introduction of machines, he can still see their usefulness. He knows that the machines are there to stay and concludes that they should be accepted and made use of. He also warns that man should keep his heart and become the master of machines and should not allow them to rule human life. Ananta urges the workers to form a union to bargain collec- tively with the factory owners for jobs and keep the old brotherhood alive. In this, he wins the support of the poet Puran Bhagat Singh. But he is unable to muster sufficient enthusiasm among the jobless, who are carried away by the demogogy of the student leader Satyapal. Events take an unexpected turn when Ralia, one of the outcasts, starts wrecking the machines. Ananta tries to stop this wanton destruction and is killed by the raging Ralia. And this is the way the novel *The Big Heart* ends.

Marlene Fisher comments :

Tha Big Heart is embodied in each scene, in each of Ananta's encounters. Because of the self he is, Ananta somehow ironically, has time—time for preparing tea for Janki, time for conversing with his poet friend, time for countless errors, time for laughter and for painful confrontations with the other coppersmiths—in short, time to live and time to die. Each such encounter within Ananta himself and with others, is organically and naturally related to those that precede and follow. Each be speaks the essential harmony and continuity as well as the many-sidedness of the character Anand has created.[5]

The basic conflict in *The Big Heart* is between tradition and modernity and this is evident in the setting of the novel. Mulk Raj Anand describes the coppersmith's lane as follows :

> It must be remembered that Billimaran is not a blind alley. Apart from the usual mouth, which even a *cul de sac* keeps open, it has another, which makes it really like a two headed snake. With one head it looks towards the ancient market, where the beautiful copper, brass, silver, and bronze utensils made in the lane are sold by dealers called Kaseras, hence called Bazar Kaserian. With the other it wriggles out towards the ironmongers Bazar, where screws and bolts and nails and locks are sold and which merges into the Booksellers' mart, the cigarette shops and the post office replete with the spirit of modern times.[6]

Further, he describes the clock tower as "the monument which ushered in the 'iron age' ... with its gigantic fourface English clock from which the families with the two or three storeyed houses in Billimaran can read the movement of the two hands of the new god, Time (p. 17).

The irony of the situation is very clear when Anand paints the picture of the people whose lives are affected by the conflict. He says :

> In the midst of this jumble of the old and the new, the men and the women of Billimaran, children, too, have assumed a different hue. They are paler and sallower, where grime and dirt does not hide their bodies. For they have to work harder they say, to buy the new gadgets of the 'iron-age' (p. 18)

Anand successfully evokes the tone of the atmosphere of Billimaran when he describes it with the note of a desperateness and sadness as if things are already out of one's control and the only way out is to wait for the tragedy. He ruminates :

Altogether, a spirit of unrest broods over Kucha Billimaran, Like the doom promised on the judgement day at
the end of the 'iron-age'. And already the convulsions
of the sad lands across the black waters are shaking this
old lane with the thunder of the machinery implanted in
its midst, which is said to be making tools for the greatest war on earth that is rumoured will be in progress at
the ends of the horizon (p. 19).

In such an atmosphere, the characters are presented
with their individual thoughts and actions and the total
fabric of the novel appears before our eyes with Ananta as
the main protagonist. The title of the novel is derived from
the oft-repeated statement of Ananta : "There is no talk of
money, brother ; one must have a big heart." And Ananta
really had a big heart and was accepted as such by most of
the people including the poet Puran Singh Bhagat. Saros
Cowasji has found a similarity between Ananta and Ratan.
He observes : "The hero Ananta, closely modelled on a
man Anand knew as a boy, has much in common with the
wrestler Ratan in *Coolie*, who speaks of the need for a big
heart."[7]

Ananta's words are, in fact, a reflection of his attitude
to life and his total philosophy towards human relationship
in such a changing society as Indian was during those days
of great upheavel and change. But more important is the
study of a character's mind as a character is portrayed from
a different angle. Mulk Raj Anand himself declared about
the portrayal of characters :

They should be portrayed as having conflicts in their
hearts and minds like the people we see around us.
They should be shown immersed in active discussion
and disruption because light can be felt only when the
darkness, which is the opposite of life is understood.
They should be depicted with all the unreasonableness
of the human heart and temperament emanating from
the unconscious.[8]

Ananta is always disturbed by the strange sounds coming from his unconscious in the form of a dream which he
had seen earlier. Throughout his life, the dream and the
images and visions of the dream throw their shadows on
the events of his life. While he is working in the midst of

the great disturbance caused by the removal of the 'Kaseras' and the introduction of machines, the conflict in the mind continues. Ananta describes the conflict in his mind as follows : "But within him there was the surging of a peculiar 'ghoon macon', a kind of disturbance spreading like knife-edges from the bits of the dream he had" (p. 20).

The dream which he had seen is like this :

> Stark silence had brooded over the cremation ground, and his mother, his dead mother, had stood burning. even as she was exhorting him to look after his step-mother Karmo. And then, suddenly, he had seen himself—was it on the platform of the railway station or the base of the clock tower ? He couldn't remember now. ... And then there was a considerable crowd before him and he had begun to speak. But Janki, his mistress, had interrupted him with a wail, and as he had turned to go towards her in a garden which looked like Guru Ka Bagh, the crowd had become like the masked men he had seen in the dacoit films in Bombay. ... And they were following him, while he had run, their hands dripping with blood. He had been frightened and had tried to run faster, but behind him there was a voice, calling, "I am hungry, I want blood !' And he had felt almost overpowered. ... He had looked back and found a black woman with a trident in her hand standing on the cremating ground, stamping upon corpses and dancing as she shrieked again and again, 'I am hungry ! I want blood' ! And he could hear the dead moaning under the feet of the woman, whom he soon recognized as Goddess Kali, for her tongue was bulging out red, and her eyes were like two sharp glintdiscs, shining like diamonds from the coal-black face. He had tried to shout for help. But no words had come from his open mouth. And he had to stand there, dazed with horror at the massacred bodies, till he saw a policeman with a machine gun coming towards him, and he had turned—to wake up in a sweat which even now trailed, down in crystals off his forehead (p. 20).

This dream follows him every time and everywhere. Though he continues to do his work, the uneasiness always lurks behind the curtain of darkness in his mind :

> He did not stop to wipe the sweat. ... An artist over and above the craftsman, his hand moved with an easy grace in spite of the disturbance within him.... But the swirl-

ing uneasines inside him rose in sudden burts of sickness and slowed him down as if, he were face to face with the black death (p. 20).

The image of Kali and then the thought of sacrifice has been very artistically presented by Anand in the form of the dream. The dream has many other reflections on the character of Ananta. It also gives hints, through the symbols, of his ambitions, desires, wishes, hopes, fears and complexes. If the dream is interpreted properly, it throws light on the coming events and the end of Ananta's life.

In fact, the novel takes a very different meaning if one can detach oneself from the very obvious theme of tradition *versus* modernity and industrialization. Anand uses a language with hidden hints that Ananta is not troubled so much by unemployment due to the introduction of machines, though this is the outer structure of the novel. Ananta is caught between the war of good and evil. His soul is in trouble and his spirit in great turmoil, and this becomes clear from the following :

A turbulent spirit and wanton in reaching out after life, he sensed now and then the pose of a furious calm in himself, like that of a leaf suddenly come still in a storm, especially after he had been struggling like a tormented beast in the cage of his soul (p. 21).
... so he drunk liquor, as well as the brakish blood of his own liver and supped on the putrid sweat sodden world around him.... 'There was quite a thick crowd of hooded men in the cremation ground,'the muttered to himself 'almost like the shadow of.... He dared not name the awful thing (p. 23).
The rising pressure of the storkes sharpened the edges of his bones with a new courage until he felt as if he were Raja Rasalu, the proverbial hero of the Punjabi legend, setting off on his adventures seated on a white charger (p. 23).

There is something strange and vision-like quality within Ananta which has baffled himself and Janki, too. She says : "There is something about you which makes people either your worst enemies or your best friends." Ananta himself realizes the fact that he has not been understood by people. He tells Janki : "I am a much misunderstood person".

We get a hint to Ananta's real identity when Anand says: "He seemed to be,... with the abandon of a prophet." Ananta is lonely because he has been isolated, though this isolation is more on the inner level than physical. It is true not only for Ananta but also for most of the central characters created by Mulk Raj Anand. Alastair Niven has the following to say about this common trait in Anand's art of characterization : "Yet the strange isolation which seems a condition of all Anand's central characters—and which makes the conflict between the individual and his community so potentially tragic a theme—has come to pervade him, bringing with it deep-rooted sadness."[9]

Ananta is very lonely amongst the people, in spite of the image of a rogue, a drunkard, a whore-monger, and immoral person, totally devoted to good food, heavy drinking and sex. But this is not the complete picture of Ananta because "He felt alone and his heart palpitated like a wild bird with flapping wings. He thought he had been caught in the trap spread by some wily invisible hunter" (p. 41).

Ananta is being prepared for the sacrificial death, very symbolically, by the demand of blood in the dream. He is misunderstood as all prophets are. He is alone as all saviours are. In the battle between good and evil, he represents the good which is going to lose only from a limited point of view. In the narrow and selfish sense, death is the greatest loss, but when the purpose and aim of life is to be taken as a service to humanity, death does not have that awful proportion which is generally attached to it. Sardar Pooran Singh Bhagat had told him never to surrender to fear but to continue" holding fast to the light which is in you, you will be so strengthened that you will go a long way—even if you don't get there". "And where does one want to get to ? "Ananta had asked." Oh, not very far, "Puran Singh Bhagat had answered. "To oneself and to others." "A long pilgrimage that—to oneself and others," Ananta muttered to himself (p. 63).

Anand describes him thus : "While his eyes stared with a rapt expression into the void before him, as though, right at the moment that he had been caught in the world of time, the timeless world had pulled him back to the eternities " (p. 68). Ananta, from the beginning is tormented because his search; which is endless, starts from within and goes to, as Puran Singh Bhagat has said, the same.

The novel is thus an effort to understand the meaning and purpose of life—to grapple with the conflict of death and immortality. Ananta dies like a prophet so that people could be saved from the doom which seems to be physical but is, in fact, spiritual. To make people understand the vision of light, to get out of the darkness of soul, he dreams of Kali wanting to drink blood. He offers blood and in death he attains immortality. Whether the end brings some kind of salvation or not, it does denote the endlessness of such a search. The dream once interpreted from this point of view of the complex working of the unconscious, makes the meaning clear that it was his blood that the Goddess wanted to drink so that others could be saved.

REFERENCES

1.   K.K. Sharma, *Perspectives on Mulk Raj Anand* (Gaziabad : Vimal Prakashan, 1978), pp. x-xi.
2.   *Ibid.*, p. xii.
3.   *Ibid* , pp. xii-xiii.
4.   K.R. Srinivasa Iyengar, *Indian Writing in English* (Bombay : Asia Publishing House, 1962), p. 258.
5.   Marlene Fisher, *The Wisdom of the Heart* (New Delhi : Sterling publishers, 1985), p. 79.
6.   Mulk Raj Anand, *The Big Heart* (New Delhi : Arnold Heinemann, 1945), pp. 16-17. All references to this work are given inside the text.
7.   Saros Cowasji, *So Many Freedoms* (Bombay : Oxford University Press, 1977), p. 127.
8.   Sharma, *Perspectives on Mulk Raj Anand*, p. xxii.
9.   Alastair Niven, *The Yoke of Pity* (New Delhi : Arnold Heinemann, 1978), p. 76,

4

The Flower-Motif in R. K. Narayan's Novels

(Mrs) S. SENGUPTA

One of the problems faced by Indian writers writing in English was to create a genuine Indian atmosphere in a foreign language. Writers tried to get over this difficulty by using various devices, sometimes linguistic and at other times cultural, and very often a happy mixture of both. Mulk Raj Anand, for example, uses literal translations of vernacular abuses and idioms in his novels, and Raja Rao uses Indian myths and legends to bring out the various aspects of Indian life. When we come to R.K. Narayan, we find that he uses not only linguistic devices but some cultural devices as well to create a flavour that is typically Indian. The use of flowers is one of them. Flowers are strewn all over the stories of his novels. They range from the rare red lotus to the wild lantana. He uses flowers to complete a domestic scene and again in the context of worship of gods and goddesses.

A careful reading of R.K. Narayan's novels shows that he has used flowers as a motif in the sense that they recur frequently in his novels. The present paper is an attempt to trace this flower-motif in his novels and to show how the jasmine evolves as a symbolic motif.

II

In one of his early novels, *The Bachelor of Arts*, Narayan reveals his attitude to flowers. There is a piquant scene of a thief stealing flowers. Chandran, along with his father and brother, wake up at four-thirty in the morning to catch the thief. The thief turns out to be a *sanyasi*. When he is accused of stealing flowers, he quitely says :

> If you lock the gate, how else can I get in than by jumping over the wall ? As for stealing flowers, *flowers are there, God-given*. What matter is whether you throw the flowers on the gods or I do it. It is all the same.[1]

To Chandran's utter bewilderment, his mother agrees with the thief :

> You can go now, sir, If you want flowers you can take them. There couldn't be a better way of worship than giving flowers to those who really worship.[2]

Thus at once a relationship has been established between flowers and the worship of gods. And this relationship gains strength and recurs in subsequent novels.

In *The Guide*, Raju's gradual transformation into a *Swami* is associated with the flower-motif. Raju's abode becomes a shrine and is decorated by the villagers with "flowers and greenery and festoons everywhere."[3] We are further informed : "They brought him huge chrysanthemum garlands, jasmine and rose petals in baskets."[4]

Similarly, in *The Financial Expert* the flower motif has been used both in the context of the domestic scene as well as in the context of worship. Margayya is shown telling a story to his son. He "...began a story of the fox, the crow and the lion, till the boy intercepted him with : 'I don't like the fox story. Tell me a flower story."[5] There is rather unusual. Children usually demand animal stories or stories about a king and his queen or fairy tales.

There is another scene later in the book where flowers are used to create a felicitous domestic atmosphere :

> After finishing all her work, his wife came up with an endearing smile and sat beside him on the mat. He put his arm round her and drew her nearer. She nestled close to him. It was as if he had thrown off twenty years and were back in the bridal chamber. He said : "Why don't you buy flowers regularly ? I see that you don't care for them nowadays."

"I am an old woman, flowers and such things —" "But this old man likes to see some flowers in this old lady's hair", he said. They laughed and felt very happy.[6]

This is one of the rare happy scenes in an otherwise unhappy novel. Margayya has plenty to worry about as "a financial expert." But when he is in a temple, "a mixed smell of oil, *flowers* and incense hung in the air. That was a combination of scent which always gave Margayya a feeling of elation. He shut his eyes. For a moment he felt that he was in a world free from all worrying problems. It was in many ways a noble world, where everything ran smoothly."[7]

Later, in his ambition to become rich, he decides to propitiate the goddess of wealth, Laxmi. And this time 'red lotus' makes its appearance, a flower associated with goddess Laxmi. But then red lotuses are not easy to find and the priest says :

...our world is going to pieces because we have no more lotus about. Its a great flower—the influence it has on a human being is incalculable.[8]

The priest asks Margayya to go beyond Sarayu, towards the North where there is a garden. In that garden there is a ruined temple with a pond. When Margayya goes there "in the middle of the pond there were lotus flowers —red as the rising sun."[9]

III

Of all flowers, the jasmine seems to hold a special place in Narayana's heart. For him jasmine is the flower of happiness. It appears as a motif but with the added dimension of a symbol—a symbol of happiness.

Jasmine as a symbol of happiness permeates *The English Teacher*. But it also occurs as a symbol in such later novels as *The Financial Expert* and *The Guide*. *The Financial Expert* is an unhappy story. It deals with family dissensions, discontent, disharmony. The first part of the novel shows us Margayya, a poor man, trying to earn money by fair means or foul. Money, he thinks, is the open seasame to all happiness. In the latter half of the book, he is presented as a wealthy man, but still happiness eludes him and his wife. Significantly enough, we do not find the mention of jasmine anywhere in the novel except once, even though other flowers abound. Only once is Balu's mother shown enjoying a modicum of happiness and then she has jasmine in her hair. Her son whom she had taken for dead, returns to her. There is joy and peace in her mind. That is the only time that jasmine makes its appearances in the novel :

> A new flush appeared on her sallow cheeks...She took the trouble to comb her hair with care and stuck jasmine strings in it. She seemed to feel that she was born a new in this world. She spoke light-heartedly and with a trembling joy in her voice.[10]

We find a similar experience in *The Guide*. Rosie has led a miserable life with her husband. Her misery is no less when she lives in Raju's house as his mistress, taunted by his mother as a whore and looked down upon by all the neighbours.

It is later when she blossoms as an artiste that she finds joy in living. Though she still lives with Raju, she is released from her bondage to him. She is a free being and, what is more, she has realized herself as an artiste— a dancer sought after by all those who cared for art. Her life is fulfilled and sure enough we find the scent of the jasmine filing the pages :

> Nalini cherished every garland that she got at the end of a performance. . .She said holding up a piece of garland and sniffing the air for the fragrance. 'To me this is the only worthwhile part of our whole activity. . . .I love jasmine."[11]

It is significant that earlier, when she lived with her husband, her dress had been described elaborately. But Narayan did not give her jasmine there. There was still a sweet smell about her but it is the scent of a perfume as artificial as the make-belief happiness with her husband. The novelist seems to suggest that she has no right to wear jasmine flowers. The jasmine is reserved for moments when the heart overflows with real happiness.

IV

It is in the *English Teacher* that jasmine as a symbol of happiness finds its finest expression. In America the book came out under the title *Grateful to Life and Death*. Krishna is very happy in his marriage with Susila and very early in the novel we have the fragrance of jasmine emanating from her letter :

> I smelt my wife's letter before opening it. It carried with it the fragrance of her trunk, in which she always kept her stationery—a mild jasmine smell surrounded her and all her possessions ever since I had known her.[12]

In fact, jasmine as a symbol has settled at the very core of the novel, Susila radiates happiness around her. So in the novel she becomes the very apotheosis of jasmine. There are numerous occasions when, brimming with happiness, Krishna calls her 'jasmine' :

> The fresh sun, morning light, the breeze and my wife's presences, who looked so lovely—even an unearthly loveliness—her tall form, dusky complexion and two small ear rings—Jasmine, Jasmine, ..."I will call you jasmine, hereafter "I said "I've long waited to tell you that ...".[13]

Jasmine as a symbol makes its presence felt even before Susila makes her appearance in the novel. Krishna, the English teacher, had grown a jasmine in the college hostel in which he lived before his wife and daughter joined him. Many persons had laughed at him for doing so :

> "Why should we grow a jasmine bush in a boy's hostel ?" I was often asked. "Just to remind us that there are better things in the world, that is all," I replied.[14]

In other words, what Narayan means to say is that in this materialistic world torn with strife, jasmine takes on a symbolic significance, expressive of not only beauty but also beatitude. Referring to the jasmine bush a little later in the novel, he calls it "The only object of beauty hereabouts." Hence his lovely wife is associated with jasmine, spreading her delicious fragrance wherever she goes :

> I studied her face without her knowledge. A great peace had descended on her. "It is God's grace that has

given me this girl." The jutka was filled with the scent of the jasmine in her hair and the glare of the indigo-coloured saree.[15]

But Susila dies of typhoid and Krishna's misery knows no bounds. The light of happiness has gone out of his life and so has the perfume of jasmine. After that, there is just one mention of jasmine in about fifty pages : Susila's dead body is being decked :

> Her [Susila's] face looks at the sky, bright with the saffron touched on her face, and the vermilion on her forehead and a string of jasmine somewhere about her head.

Jasmine goes out of his life for sometime, as does Susila and with them all his happiness.

He is distraught. Life does not hold any meaning for him any longer :

> The days had acquired a peculiar blankness and emptiness.[16]

This mechanical existence continues for some time till he is able to establish contact with his dead wife through a medium. He is filled with new life and vigour :

> Nowadays I went about my work with a light heart. I felt as if a dead load had been lifted, The day seemed full of possibilities of surprise and joy. At home I devoted myself to my studies more energetically. The sense of futility was leaving me.[17]

Immediately after this the jasmine makes its reappearance. This is how Susila describes her dress, speaking from 'the bourne of the untravelled country from which no traveller returns' :

> My dress to night is a shimmering blue, ink blue inter-woven with light and stars. I have done my hair parted on the left. (And what a load of jasmine and other rare flowers I have in my hair for your sake).[18]

The sub-plot of the novel also depicts the life of a teacher, in this case, the headmaster of a school. It is interesting to note that jasmine is not mentioned anywhere in the sub-plot because it deals with the marital discord of the headmaster and his wife. The headmaster's family life is in sharp contrast to Krishna's. It is marked by abuses and dissensions. While presenting this contrastive picture, the novelist seems to be trying to make us taste both heaven and hell, the beautiful and the ugly, the fragrance and the stink of life.

Thus, in the ultimate analysis, jasmine becomes a *leit-motif* in the novel, a chord struck early in symphony and struck again and again, increasing intensity during the course of the novel, each time gathering new meaning and new significance till at the end of the book it ascends in a crescend when "past, present and the future weild into one."

One night, Krishna returns from a farewell-party with a garland of jasmine round his arm. He hangs it in his room. Very soon the whole house is permeated with the fragrance of flowers, and he finds the atmosphere "sur-charged with strange spiritual forces." It is an ecstatic experience and gradually he realizes the presence of his wife, whom death has not been able to snatch away from him. There is a divine beauty about her heightened by the jasmine in her hair :

I gazed on her face. There was an over-whelming frag-rance of jasmine surrounding her. "Still jasmine-scented ! "I commented".[19]

And as they stood grazing on the first purple of the dawn, the boundaries of their personality seemed to dissolve and they were one :

It was a moment of rare immutable joy—a moment for which one feels *grateful to Life and Death*'.[20]

The original title of the book is vindicated. And so is Naray n use of flowers as motif in his novels.

REFERENCES

1. *The Bachelor of Arts* (Mysore : Indian Thought Fublications, 1961), p. 43.
2. *Ibid.,* p. 44.
3. *The Guide* (Mysore : Indian Thought Publications, 1958), p. 43.
4. *Ibid.,* p. 79.
5. *The Financial Expert* (Michigan State College Press, 1953), p. 74.

6. *Ibid.*, p. 73.
7, *Ibid.*, p. 38.
8. *Ibid.*, p. 48.
9. *Ibid.*, P. 51.
10. *Ibid.*, p. 143.
11. *The Guide*, p. 173.
12. *The English Teacher* (Mysore : Indian Thought Publications, 1953), p. 19.
13. *Ibid.*, p. 51.
14. *Ibid.*, p. 20.
15. *Ibid.*, p. 113.
16. *Ibid.*, p. 116.
17. *Ibid.*, p. 145.
18. *Ibid.*, p. 161.
19. *Ibid.*, p. 228.
20. *Ibid.*

5
Raja Rao : A Reappraisal

K.K. SHARMA

The Indian English novel proper came into being in the 'thirties with the advent of the 'big three'—Mulk Raj Anand, R.K. Narayan and Raja Rao. To-day, besides these three who are doubtless among the great novelists of the world, there are fictionists like Bhabani Bhattacharya, Manohar Malgonkar. Kamala Markandaya and Anita Desai who have achieved global fame. But as I consider Raja Rao as the most outstanding Indian novelist writing in English, the present paper is an attempt to set forth the achievements of this novelist, without being indifferent to his weaknesses. In fact, my endeavour will be to evaluate the mind and art of Raja Rao as dispassionately as possible, and to highlight his contribution to the Indian English novel in particular and the novel in general.

Despite his small corpus of literary output—just five novels and one collection of short stories—and his extremely complex creative genius, Raia Rao is acknowledged as a great writer of fiction the world over. His literary genius is shaped by many influences, some of which are invaluable to the adequate understanding of his works. Perhaps the most important formative influence on him was that of his grand father, Ramakrishna, who was a Vedantin out and out, and it was he who taught him the *Upanishads* and *Amara* at the age of five. Incidentally, this Vedantin novelist was born at the very moment when his father was offering lemon to the Vedantin-king of Mysore, Krishna Raja, after whom he was named Raja. Thus Vedantin and Indian philosophy he inherited by birth. His higher studies in History and Philosophy, both Indian and Western, further shaped his creative mind. Gandhiji's tremendous impact on his young impressionable mind in the 'thirties also conditioned his writings. Above all, his intimacy with, and submission to, his Guru Sri Atmananda contributed most to his philosophic vision which finds artistic expression in his writings. While studying his works, we should also take into account the French literary world of the 'thirties, dominated by Valéry, Gide and others, in which he chanced to live to pursue his doctoral research. Lastly, he was greatly fascinated by the famous Kannada saint-poet of his region, Kanakadas, who represented the typical Indian creative tradition—poetic-philosophic-social —some four hundred years ago.

II

Raja Rao has his own conception of literature and the writer, which, though based on the great ancient Indian tradition, is universal, and therefore is reflected also in the art and ideas of the immortal Europeans like Valéry, Rilke, Kafka and others. He is of the view that literature is an embodiment of *Sadhana*, a spiritual experience, and that the writer's creative act stems from his dedication to metaphysics. Elucidating his notion of literature as *sadhana*, he writes :

So the idea of literature as anything but a spiritual experience or *sadhana*—a much better word—is outside my perspective. I really think that only through dedication to the absolute or metaphysical Principle can one be fully creative,

Literature as *sadhana* is the best life for a writer. The Indian tradition which links the world with the absolute (*Sabdabrahman*) has clearly shown the various ways by which one can approach literature, without the confusions that arise in the mind of the Western writer viewing life as an intellectual adventure. Basically, the Indian outlook follows a deeply satisfying, richly rewarding and profoundly metaphysical path.

All this may sound terribly Indian, but it is not so really. Valéry, Rilke, and Kafka, for instance, are as close to this view as Tagore in looking upon literature as *sadhana*.[1]

By *sadhana*, Raja Rao means a kind of spiritual discipline and growth, or a sort of complete devotion to the metaphysical being. The writer, according to him, as essentially a man, striving to have a metaphysical entity. The writer attains this state of higher being by seeking the guidance of a Guru and by living lonely in silence. And when he gets the spiritual realisation, he feels the compulsion to express it. It is in this way that literature is created and such a literature is for the writer's own sake, or *swanta hsukhai* (self-pleasure), as the great Hindi saint-poet Tulsidas calls it. When the author is able to merge his identity into the Metaphysical Being, he does not bother about his name, and hence the ancient tradition of anonymity.

III

Raja Rao's central preoccupation in his writings is with India. His attitude towards India is well expressed in these words of Ramaswamy : My India I carried wherever I went"[2] and "India is the Guru of the world, or She is not India."[3] Like Ramaswamy, he believes that India is everywhere "wheresoever you see, hear, touch, taste, smell."[4] Raja Rao is so completely preoccupied by Indianness that even Comrade Kirillov, who is a devotee of Communism and Russia, is "an Indian—and his Indianhood would break through every communist chain."[5]

The focal point of Raja Rao's Indianness is the ancient Indian philosophy which forms the core of his fictional works. *Kanthapura* deals, in detail, with the *karma* philosophy, which is the commonplace of Indian thought. In its abstract form it finds its most lucid and authentic expression in the *Gita*, while in its concrete and practical form it is best expressed in the ideas and actions of Gandhiji. Thus it is not surprising that Gandhiji is at the centre of the book, and it is rightly described as Gandhi-*purana*.

The Serpent and the Rope is perhaps the greatest metaphysical novel written in the English language. It is an artistic exposition of the highest school of Indian philosophy, the *Advaita* of Sri Sankara. The central theme of the novel is the Indian idea of the Absolute, the Truth, the Ultimate Reality or Substance of the universe, which is distinguishable from the relative, the illusion or the shadow. This is explained, in detail, through the well-known analogy of the serpent and the rope, thoroughly treated by Sri Sankaracharya in his enunciation of the *Advaita* philosophy. A Vedantist, Raja Rao stresses that man must not mistake the relative for the Absolute, the illusion for the Reality, the particular for the Universal, the moment for the Eternity, the shadow for the substance, the rope for the serpent. The novel accentuates the Indian conviction that man can comprehend this discrimination between illusion and reality, and that the illusory world vanishes through the true knowledge, especially the knowledge of the Self which is attainable in its true form only with the help of the Guru.

In *The Cat and Shakespeare* which is a teasingly complex work of fiction, Raja Rao focusses on a particular school of the Vedanta philosophy called *Vishistadvaita* which prescribes its own method of achieving the Truth or Ultimate Reality, that is, love to God and becoming one with *Brahman*. This philosophical doctrine, authentically interpreted by Ramanuja in the eleventh centuty, is radically different from the *Advaita* of Sankara. While the latter stresses *Jnana Yoga*, the path of knowledge, the former emphasizes *Bhakti Yoga*, the path of love and devotion. Ramanuja expounded the doctrine of the *prapatti* or self-surrender by which he does not mean the extinction of self, but the union of the will of man with the will of God. Later on, Ramanuja's doctrine of man's complete dependence on God was interpreted in two different ways resulting in two philosophical schools. The first, propounding the *markata-nyaya*—The Monkey-theory— points out that man endeavours to realise the Supreme Reality by his own free will and endeavours to do so in the manner in which the young monkey clings to its mother. On the other hand, the second school, expounding the *marjaranyaya*, the cat-hold-theory, preaches that man can become one with the Ultimate Reality by remaining passive and helpless like a kitten before the mother cat. As the cat safely carries its kitten by scruff of the neck, so *Brahman*, or the Absolute preserves the man who surrenders himself completely to Him. In *The Cat and Shakespeare*, Raja Rao prefers the cat-hold-theory to the monkey theory and discusses it in an artistic manner through the thoughts and actions of the two prominent characters in the novel, Govindan Nair and Ramakrishna Pai.

Like his other novels, Raja Rao's *Comrade Kirillov* is saturated with philosophy. It examines some of the basic philosophical thoughts, Indian as well as Western—viz. Theosophy, Gandhism, Vedantism, Communism, etc. But it mainly concentrates upon Marxism, though it shows the superiority of Vedantism over it. The hero of the novel, Comrade Kirillov, who is an intellectual spiritual youngman, is a thirsty soul pinning for the attainment of the higher truths and is given to meditations and serious thinking.

Raja Rao's recently published novel, *The Chessmaster and His Moves* again embodies his abstract quest for the Absolute, and belies the belief that the twentieth-century man is obsessed with only materialism. This voluminous work touches almost all the subjects under the sun, ranging from God to a wretch on this earth, from the sublime to the ordinary, from violence to non-violence, from monarchy to democracy, from fascism to anarchism, from Hinduism to other religious 'isms', etc. ; but the basic theme, viz. the search for the Absolute, is never kept out of vision. The hero-narrator of the novel, Sivarama Sastri, a young Brahmin, Vedantin-mathematician, goes to Paris for further research ; but, like Ramaswamy of *The Serpent and the Rope*, he is throughout possessed with the quest for the Absolute. No wonder in a chat with Dr. Jean-Pierre, he asserts : "the Absolute in fact can only be indicated by symbols and silences—the frozen lake, the dip the untouched wings of the Cygne—they gave meaning to life, death and immortality."[5] True, Sivarama Sastri is a mathematician with an extraordinary urge to find a solution to the problem of attaining the Absolute or the Ultimate for which he uses variegated equations and undertakes several psycho-analytical exercises. Though he reposes full faith in Sri

Sankara's theory of non-dualism, yet he does not hesitate in drawing nectar from other branches of oriental philosophy.

In short, the fountain-head of Raja Rao's creative impulse is the rich philosophical heritage of India.

IV

Owing to India's close contacts with the Western countries for centuries, a patent feature of Indian English literature is the treatment of the East-West encounter. Thus most of the celebrated Indian English novelists have explored the varied aspects of the East-West theme in their creative writings. Raja Rao's novels are of great interest in this regard, for they examine thoroughly the dissimilarity, contrast, conflict and oneness of the East and the West at various levels: political, philosophical, religious and spiritual. While *Kanthapura* and *The Cow of the Barricades* deal with the political and social facets of the theme superficially, the two novels – *The Serpent and the Rope* and *Comrade Kirillov*—comprehensively treat the theme in its variegated aspects : religious, philosophical, spiritual, intellectual, etc.

Like D.H. Lawrence, Raja Rao is deeply concerned with one of the fundamental realities of human life, viz., the man-women relationship. His novels, especially *The Serpent and the Rope* and *The Cat and the Shakespeare*, probe the mysteries of the Femine Principle, revealing its basic nature and its various facets. The hero discovers in the woman of his choice a chemical mixture of mistress, whore, child and mother; he finds her sexual, strong, compassionate, sensitive, intelligent and mysterious. In his fiction, the novelist repeatedly portrays the sense of mystery that distinguishes the two sexes but exalts both. Though speaking of his sister Saroja, Ramaswamy expresses his belief in the incomprehensible mystery of woman : "What a deep and reverential mystery womanhood is."[7] However, despite his conviction that woman is an unsolved mystery, hs discerns in her the never-changing truth, the abiding reality. This is explicit from what he says about his unique experience with Savithri.

Raja Rao thinks that it is through woman that man can fully know and realise himself. Man finds in woman an amalgam of sensuality and spirituality, Evidently, Raja Rao holds woman in high esteem. He considers her the noblest and purest incarnation of the elements that constitute human life. She is the inevitable reality, and is absolutely essential for the well-being of man—physical, emotional, intellectual and spiritual. No wonder Raja Rao goes into raptures when he poetically describes the significance of woman in the world :

Woman is the earth, air, ether, sound; woman is the microcosm of the mind, the articulations of space, the knowing in knowledge ; the woman is fire, movement clear and rapid as the mountain stream ; the woman is that which seeks against that which is sought. To Mitra she is Varuna, to Indra she is Agni, to Rama she is Sita, to Krishna she is Radha. Woman is the meaning of the word, the breath, touch, act ; woman, that which reminds man of that which he is, and reminds herself through him of that which she is. Woman is kingdom, solitude, time ; woman is growth, the gods, inherence ; the woman is death, for it is through woman that one is born ; woman rules, for it is she the universe. She is the daughter of the earth, the queen, and it is to her that elephant and horse, camel, deer, cow and peacock bow that she reign over us, as in some medieval Book of Hours where she is clad in the blue of the sky. . . .

Woman is the world. Woman is the earth and the cavalcade, the curve of the cloud and the round roundness of the sun. Woman is the space between mansions. . . .[8]

More than Dickens, Emile Bronte, George Eliot, Tolstoy, Hemingway and Mulk Raj Anand, Raja Rao is autobiographical in his writings. Like D.H. Lawrence, he projects himself artistically in his fictional characters. Consequently, there is usually a close resemblance between him and his protagonists. Ramaswamy's following assertion in *The Serpent and the Rope* is a spontaneous expression of Raja Rao's belief that literature is essentially autobiographical :

. . . . all books are autobiographies, whether they be
books on genetics on the history (in twenty-two volumes)
of the Anglican Church. The mechanics of a motorcar
or of veterinary science all have a beginning in the
man who wrote the book, have absorbed his nights and
may be the nerves of his wife or daughter. They all
represent a bit of oneself, and for those who can read
rightly, the whole of oneself.[9]

In fact, the whole of Raja Rao, with his likes and dislikes, passions and thoughts, is present in his fiction. His
writings are a record of the variegated facets of his life :
emotional, intellectual, moral, spiritual, etc. ; they vividly
portray some of the salient traits of his personality and
almost all the major events of his life. There is an obvious
resemblance between him and his characters. Like him, all
his heroes from Moorthy to Comrade Kirillov are South
Indian Brahmins who are profoundly in love with India and
her philosophy, and are truly in search of truth and *Brahman*.
They are staunch believers and champions of the *Advaita*
philosophy, with the exception of Moorthy who is a devotee
of Gandhism and the *Karma* philosophy. Like the novelist,
two of his four heroes are destined to live in the West for a
long time, but they never forget their country and her immensely rich cultural heritage. Thus Raja Rao is a novelist
who continually attempts to externalise his own self and is
present in his writings.

V

Though fully familiar with the modern Westwern novel
marked by a lot of experimentation, Raja Rao is not interested in giving a strikingly new form or structure to the
novel. He is essentially Indian in regard to the form of his
novels; they are very close to the Indian *Purana* and *folk
epic*. *Kanthapura* is called *Sthalapurana* and *The Serpent
and the Rope*, a *Mahapurana*. A Purana, which is an old
Indian form of literature, is an amalgam of history, totality
of existence, philosophical reflections on life and religion,
stories, fables, legends, long poetic descriptions of places
and nature, mystical experiences, observations on ideolo-

gies. etc. *Kanthapura*, "a rich Sthala-Purana, a legendary history", is crammed with a large number of episodes in the manner of the *Mahabharata*, the *Ramayana* and the *Puranas*.

Though epical in form and crammed with episodes, many of which appear digressions at times, *The Serpent and the Rope* has considerable structural unity. It is verily a *Mahapurana* or a major epic legend, having a wonderful width of sweep. Commenting on the form of the book, Raja Rao observes that it "is to be taken like all my writings as an attempt at a 'Puranic' recreation of Indian story telling: that is to say, the story as story is conveyed through a thin thread to which are attached (or which passes through) many other stories, fables and philosophical disquisitions, like a *mala*."[20]

The Cat and Shakespeare possesses a highly complex but compact structure. In spite of the baffling obscurity and incoherence of meaning and style, everything in the book has a relevance to its meaning and form. The various images, myths, phrases, dialogues, symbols, events, characters, etc. are organised in such an artistic way as to give the novel a unique richness of meaning and form. Above all, it is the novelist's use of the central symbol of the house that gives the book a rare unity. Raja Rao's novel *Comrade Kirillov*, however, reveals a decline in his power of construction. It is a record of the various events in the life of Comrade Kirillov and of the transitions of his thoughts. Unfortunately, these are not linked together adequately, and if there is anything unifying in the narrative, it is only the personality of the protagonist dominating it from the beginning to the end. Irene's diary entries are also not closely connected with the main narrative; they are just digressions, though they throw light on the internal as well as the external life of the hero. Obviously, the novel is episodic in structure and badly lacks architectural design. Unlike the author's other novels, it does not make an extensive use of symbols, myths and legends, which might have enriched its meaning and given it a compact structure. The same may be said, to a large degree, about *The Chessmaster and His Moves* which does not possess a traditional strucrure at all.

VI

As a novelist, Raja Rao's *forte* is the portrayal of character, and in this his fecundity and creative power is just amazing. Indeed, it is not his exposition of Indian philosophy or his treatment of varied themes, but his creation of living characters which makes him a great creative artist. Some of the people in his fiction are undoubtedly most deeply realised characters, and the chief among them are Moorthy, Ramaswamy, Govindan Nair, Ramakrishna Pai, Madeleine Shantha, Comrade Kirillov, Irene Suvarama Sastri, Uma, Jayalakshmi Suzanne and Mireille. Raja Rao paints not merely what D.H. Lawrence calls man's stable ego, but also his *alter ego*, the other self—viz., the inner side of his being.

A conspicuous feature of Raja Rao's major characters is that they are highly intellectual. Then, he draws ideal characters. Consequently, at times they appear to be mere ideas and fail to become "the whole man alive". Despite their remarkable learning and idealism, some of Raja Rao's heroes are extremely complex and paradoxical, having a number of contradictory traits. Ramaswamy, who is one of the most philosophical characters in fiction, is genuinely devoted to Sri Sankara's *Advaita*; but at the same time he is a sensualist. In Moorthy, Ramaswamy and Comrade Kirillov, we clearly perceive inconsistencies and the conflict of commitments.

An important aspect of Raja Rao's art of characterisation is his method of presenting characters in contrast. This method has been particularly employed in painting women. Thus Ratna widely differs from most of the other women in the novel. Madeleine and Savithri are at poles apart from each other. Likewise, Saroja and Shantha in *The Cat and Shakespeare* present a beautiful contrast. Lastly, it can be said that Raja Rao is endowed with an androgynous creative mind, and therefore is capable of depicting human life truthfully. Not only this, he fully succeeds in creating living men and women. He is as much skilful in drawing lifelike men as lifelike women.

VII

Raja Rao adapts the age-old Indian art of story-telling to the modern experiments made by the European novelists, and unquestionably evinces a rare skill in the handling of the narrative technique. Unlike most of the great novelists, he has used only the internal point of view of "I" as the narrator, which is well-known as the first-person singular or autobiographical mode of narration, in all the novels he has published till now. But he makes several variations on this established technique of story-telling in his different works with a view to achieving the effect of verisimilitude and authenticity.

Kanthapura is written from the point of view of "I" as witness. Achakka, a simple, old village women, is the witness-narrator. In *The Serpent and the Rope*, the novelist employs the narrative method of "I" as protagonist. Ramaswamy, a highly intellectual and sophisticated youngman, is absolutely suitable to the role of the protagonist-narrator of a story dealing with a philosophical subject matter. *The Cat and Shakespeare* shows Raja Rao's masterly use of the first-person singular point of view. The author successfully uses the technique of the protagonist-narrator-cum-witness-narrator. That is to say, Ramakrishna Pai, who is the narrator in the novel, is both the protagonist-narrator and the witness-narrator. He narrates not only the events of his own life, but also those of the life of his friend and neighbour, Govindan Nair.

In *Comrade Kirillov*, Raja Rao resorts to the device of the witness-narrator point of view. But what differentiates it from *Kanthapura* and other novels using this technical device is that it has two witness—narrators, and not one. The first and main witness—narrator is R., who is a true Vedantist and a Gandhian, and who is a relation and a close friend of the principal character, Padmanabha Iyer who later on becomes a communist and is called Comrade Kirillov. The second witness-narrator is Irene, the wife of Comrade Kirillov. Raja Rao's latest novel, *The Chessmaster and His Moves*, is mostly written from the point of view of the protagonist-narrator. What is particularly striking about it is the author's remarkable use of the stream of consciousness technique, perhaps employed by him for the first time in his long illustrious literary career. The thought-content of this novel has deeper meanings, and the level of consciousness shifts suddenly and the topic changes abruptly, with the result that the reader often feels baffled and finds it difficult to catch up with the thought—current. The technical device of the stream of consciousness is best suited to the zigzag flow of Sivarama Sastri's thoughts ranging from amorously romantic to the most sublime, from pure mathematics to metaphysics and *Vedanta*, and from *Bhaktirasa* to contemporary Indian and Western political scenes. An important aspect of Raja Rao's narrative technique is the extensive use of symbols, myths and legends. The novelist employs them in all of his writings, and through them he not only fully explores and communicates his vision of life, his theme, but also gives a compact form to his book.

VIII

Raja Rao has thought much about the problem of appropriate language of expression. When he began his literary career in the thirties, it was after a good deal of serious consideration that he decided to write in the English language. He wanted to adapt it to Indian sensibility and his own demands. He attempted to adjust it to the Indian emotional make-up and thus to transform it into Sanskritic English. He was inspired to do so by the example of the Irish writers like Yeats, James Joyce and others who created an Irish English to suit their purposes. Explaining his view on this point he writes in the Foreword to *Kanthapura*:

We are all instinctively bilingual, many of us writing in our own language and in English. We cannot write like the English. We should not. We cannot write only as

Indians. We have grown to look at the large world as part of us. Our method of expression therefore has to be a dialect which will someday prove to be as distinctive and colourful as the Irish or the American. Time alone will justify it.[11]

Flexibility is the hallmark of Raja Rao's language, and naturally he easily adapts it to the personality of his narrators and the varied situations. In *Comrade Kirillov* there are three main characters—the narrator R., Comrade Kirillov and Irene—with different temperaments, faiths and intellectual make-up. Naturally, we have three different styles in this novel. Evidently, Raja Rao's fiction reveals him as an originator and master of Indian English, and in this connection his achievement is greater than that of R. K. Narayan or Mulk Raj Anand.

IX

Like any creative writer, Raja Rao is not immune from weaknesses. A serious, popular charge against him is that he is too much philosophical, and thus his later novels cease to be novels and appear to be hardly anything more than metaphysical and moral treatises, lacking in human interest. Mulk Raj Anand spearheads this type of sharp criticism against Raja Rao's fiction. Raja Rao's preoccupation with philosophy gives rise to a few more faults. First, it makes his work obscure and difficult. Secondly, it restricts the scope for observation, invention and narration—the threefold power of a great novelist. Thirdly, it at times makes characters look mere mouthpieces of the author. Fourthly, it leaves little scope for humour which undoubtedly lends a rare charm to a work of fiction. Lastly, there is nothing original about the philosophy which forms the subject matter of his writings.

In his approach to literature and the writer, Raja Rao gives utmost importance to spiritual fulfilment or metaphysical entity. But a scrutiny of his works and life reveals insincerety and contradiction in him. Even his *magnum opus, The Serpent and the Rope*, which, as he says, "came as a result of spiritual fulfilment—that is to say it was born after I had met my Guru,"[12] fails to present the hero-narrator, Ramaswamy, who projects the author to a great extent, as a truly metaphysical being. This remarkable fictional character is spiritual only in thoughts and talks, and not in his actual life. He is captivated by Madeleine's physical lush loveliness more than by her intellectuality or spirituality. Then without any sense of guilt or pricks of conscience, he is a faithless husband and indulges in sexual acts with Savithri and Lakshmi.

Like his fictional characters, the novelist is insincere in his real life and is far from *sadhana*. He went to France to complete his doctoral research but failed to do so. He married a French girl and lived in France for many years, while he continually thought and wrote about India's glorious cultural heritage. Now when he has been mostly living in America for the last several years, obviously for the sake of money, he is still talking a lot about India and her wonderful culture and philosophy. The gulf between his thoughts and actions is evident in that he talks and writes about man's metaphysical entity, but even after getting some sort of spiritual fulfilment under the guidance of his Guru Sri Atmananda he has married an American actreas, Katherine, who lives in New York, while he resides in Texas with his son, cooking his own meals himself. Like Ramaswamy, he seems to me a wayward intellectual-sensualist, who is not able to choose his way of life finally.

Besides, Raja Rao's cogitations upon literature as *sadhana* do not hold true in the case of all great writers, Indian or Western. For instance, Kalidas, the greatest Sanskrit creative writer, and Jai Shanker Prasad, the great modern Hindi writer, though philosophical, have not written as a result of *sadhana*, spiritual fulfilment or devotion. Likewise, the greatest Western writer, Shakespeare, has not produced his plays to express his metaphysical entity, and his matchless literature is surely not the consequence of any spiritual fulfilment.

Notwithstanding these weaknesses, Raja Rao is indubitably a great novelist. In his defence much can be said. First, his fiction, though highly philosophical, is not devoid of human interest ; it gives due consideration to love, lust, marriage, social corruption, varied human relationships and political interests. Secondly, his characters are absorbing, and they are portrayed both internally and externally with greater emphasis on their *alter ego*, the inner self. Thirdly, his fiction is difficult, but it is not as difficult and puzzling as the works of James Joyce, Virginia Woolf and Faulkner. Fourthly, if poetry can be highly philosophical and religious like Milton's *Paradise Lost*, Tulsidas's *Ramcharitra Manasa*, T.S. Eliot's *Four Quartets* and Jai Shanker Prasad's *Kamayani*, then the novel can also deal with metaphysical and religious subjects. Lastly, Raja Rao's fiction is in conformity with his belief that "the Indian novel can only be epic in form and metaphysical in nature".[13]

In conclusion, it may be said that Raja Rao is a significant modern novelist, who has evinced a refreshingly fresh approach to the novel and has created a new variety of it, viz., a truly Indian novel with its roots deeply embedded in native tradition. He has made immense contribution to the growth of the novel by infusing into it philosophical depth, symbolic richness, epic breadth of vision, poetic fervour, and Indianness of style. The most Indian among Indian English writers, the most brilliant symbolist, myth-maker and philosophical novelist, and one of the finest original voices in modern fiction, Raja Rao is unquestionably one of the greatest novelists of the world today.

REFERENCES

1. S.V.V., "Raja Rao", *The Illustrated Weekly of India* (January 5, 1964), pp. 44-5.
2. *The Serpent and the Rope* (New Delhi : Orient Paperbacks, 1968), p. 376.
3. *Ibid.*, p. 332.
4. *Ibid.*, p. 389.
5. *Comrade Kirillov* (New Delhi : Orient Paperbacks, 1976), p. 91.
6. *The Chessmaster and His Moves* (New Delhi : Vision Books Pvt. Ltd., 1988). p. 25.
7. *The Serpent and the Rope*, p. 50.
8. *Ibid.*, pp., 352-53.
9. *Ibid.*, p. 166.

10. Quoted in M.K. Naik, *"The Serpent and the Rope,* : The Indo-Anglian Novel as Epic Legend/in *Critical Essays on Indian Writing in English,* ed. M.K. Naik, S.K. Desai and G.S. Amur (Madras : The Macmillan Co. of India Ltd., 1977), pp. 1-3.

11. *Kanthapura* (New Delhi : Orient Paperbacks), p. 5.

12. S.V.V., "Raja Rao", The *Illustrated Weekly of India* (January 5, 1964), p. 44,

13. Quoted in Ahmed Ali, "Illusion and Reality : The Art and Philosophy of Raja Rao", *The Journal of Commonwealth Literature* (July, 1968), p. 20.

6

Archetypal Experience in
The Serpent and the Rope

(Mrs) S. SIVARAMAN

Raja Rao's *The Serpent and the Rope* has been singled out for praise by critics as a unique work which offers a total vision of life. The rich heritage of the Indian consciousness is evoked and experienced by the central character, Ramaswamy, while he responds simultaneously to a variety of cultures and civilisations. It would not be an exaggeration to say that in Ramaswamy we have a character who has an unlimited capacity for prayer, wonder and ecstacy. His sense of identity, feeling of harmony and zest for life are what make him a worthy model for emulation, the model who had been lost sight of in the rationalisation of modern times. His healthy response to his heritage makes him rather a unique character, who reminds us of the original men whose sustaining springs never dried up. Through Ramaswamy Raja Rao brings the immemorial tradition of the whole men quite up-to-date.

Since Plato, the word archetype has been used in the sense of a pattern or model used in creation—an original form or experience which repeats itself every now and then. Mythology, folktale and religion attempt to relate the non-human world of physical nature with the human world where a God—human in shape and character—is identified with something in nature like the sun, sea or the mountain. This assimilation of all outer sense experiences to inner, psychic events was not only a primitive need but is often the main source of solace and stability in all human experience. By means of words, similes and metaphors, literature attempts what mythology attempts and becomes a direct descendent of mythology.[1] By alluding to archetypes or patterns of potential experience as encountered in stories, myths and symbols, a writer keeps the past and the present, the inner and the outer, the primitive and the modern connected and helps in attaining a whole vision.

Raja Rao's *The Serpent and the Rope,* published in 1960 and awarded the Sahitya Akademi prize in 1963, is not only his *magnum opus* but has a certain uniqueness which qualifies it to be considered a classic in Indian Writing in English. This uniqueness lies in the fact that this novel gives the experience of a full and complete "engagement of the deeper levels of personality"[2] through a symbolic language in which inner experience, feeling and thought are expressed as if they were sensory experiences—events in the outer world. Raja Rao aspires and attempts to recognise what is divine in us by evoking old myths and stories of the Indian culture. He brings the ancient "tradition quite up-to-date, to the present, to himself and the faith by which he 'feels' them in him."[3] To feel and experience what men had felt ages ago is what it means to be a representative of a culture, a group or community and Raja Rao's *The Serpent and the Rope* is the "finest and fullest expression of a profound Indian sensibility"[4] which, though it evokes the spirit of a place or a time, transcends both and captures "a continuity, a palimpsest, layer after layer of which points to the authenticity of its timelessness and pervasiveness."[5]

Raja Rao's novel is full of a heightened awareness of life. After his sojourn in Europe, returning to India on hearing about this father's illness and subsequent death, Ramaswamy, the narrator of the novel, is quick to the magic of his Indian heritage. Reciting a hymn by the sage Sankara he slips into a 'serious mood that fills him in the vastness of India.' "We feel large and infinite, compassion touching our sorrow as eyelashes touch the skin. Someone behind and beyond all living things gave us the touch, the tear, the elevation that make our natural living so tender."[6]

The Serpent and the Rope is full of the magic of poetry, the thrill of mystique experience which brings memories of a chain of endless other such men and instances when truths about human existence, life and divinity had flashed themselves upon the "inward eye." Moving towards Haridwar with little mother, as the train carried them towards the holy, the holy Himalayas, Ramaswamy experiences the thrill experienced by his Aryan ansestors. He writes :

> It was thither, when the work in the plains was over, or when one needed the integrity of selfness, that my Aryan ancestors went up the Ganges to seek the solitude of the snows and the identity of Truth. Somewhere over against the sky should Kailas stand, and Shiva and Parvathi besport themselves therein, for the joy of mankind. Nandi, the vehicle and disciple of Shiva, that bull without blemish, would wander round the world, hearing the sorrows of this vast countryside, hearing of painful birth and death, of litigation, quarrel and paupery. Parvathi would know of it, for Nandi would never dare tell his master in speech, and Parvathi would plead with Shiva that orphan, beggar and widow should have the splendour of life given unto them. You never knew when the door would open, and the sack of gold be found at your threshold (p. 35).

Transcending the limits of modern India by the use of myth, Raja Rao has created the interior landscape which links the timeless with time. As John B. Alphonso Karkala has pointed out, "Whenever a writer chooses to make use of myths, large themes, high motives, variety of symbols, the matrix of his work does in fact develop a depth and width in time and space. . . and becomes a classic in world literature."[7]

Though Ramaswamy's (and Raja Rao's) formidable imaginative ability to participate in the whole stems out of his Indian and Brahmin traditional background, it is definitely not just provincial or partisan. "There was a sainthood about the elevation of the mountain," (p. 54) whether it is the Himalayas or Mont Sainte—Victorre, and it "carried such a message of strength, and of the possible" that wherever Ramaswamy happened to be he heard Parvati singing to Shiva.

The creative participation in his own tradition gives Raja Rao's writing a sense of identity and rootedness, the lack of which is conspicuous in the modern world. Ramaswamy, the peace-loving Brahmin protagonist of *The Serpent and the Rope* loves rivers and lakes and, like an essential brahmin, is ready to make his home easily by any waterside hamlet. He is an embodiment of the essential simplicity, the refined sensibility and the nobility of a true Brahmin. Going down the banks of the Ganges he is receptive to its divine energy, compassion, force and purity. He captures the mystical experience of those Upanishadic sages who had arrived at an eternal truth on its banks. The mystic and poetic truth of the Sanskrit verse

   "*Devi Sureshwari Bhagvati Gange*"

hits him hard and he instantly feels strongly the presence of the compassionate one Himself coming down the footpath by the Saraju to wash the mendicant. If the Himalaya was like Lord Shiva himself, "distant, inscrutable, and yet very intimate" (p. 42), Ganga is Mother Ganga with her sweet motherliness "that one was unhappy to quit. . .for she it was, from age to age, who had borne the sorrows of our sorrowful land. Like one of our own mothers, Ganga, Mother Ganga, had sat by the ghats, her bundle beside her" (p. 33), The picture glows with the feeling of the author. All archetypal experiences are stirring and are capable of "evoking all those beneficial forces that have enabled mankind to find a rescue from every hazard and to outlive the longest night."[8] Ganga is also the 'Gyana Ganga', the knowledge that cuts across time and space and flows eternally in the veins of man provoking a sense of holiness and happiness.

Among mystic patterns the rebirth archetype is at the centre and its influence on the human mind cannot be dismissed easily. The truth inherent in life, the truth that the cycle of death and birth goes on eternally like the snows and the rivers comes, home to Ramaswamy on the banks of the Ganges. If the Ganges held the secrets of existence, Benares proclaims the deathlessness of man : "In Benares one knows death is as illusory as the mist in the morning. The Ganges is always there" (p. 11).

All water is identified with the archetypal Ganga and all those who experiences the truth within themselves, the sadhus, are identified with the archetypal Shiva : "Sadhus by their fires, lost in such beautiful magnanimity, as though love were not something that one gave to another, but what one gave to oneself. His trident in front of him, his holy books open...each Sadhu sat, a Shiva" (p. 12). Quoting from Sankara's *Nirvanashtakam* later Shiva is identified with the self :

*"Manobuddhi ahankara cittani naham
Cidananda rupah Shivoham—Shivoham"*

(I am not the mind, I am neither Intelligence nor egoism, I am joy of intelligence—I am Shiva—I am Shiva).

Innumerable instances of the protagonist's capacity to wonder and thrill and healthily respond to his environment are to be found in *The Serpent and the Rope*. The blooming of womanhood in his sister Saroja intoxicates him so that he experiences the "primordial awakening in a creature" similar to the "new moon or the change of equinox, having polar affinities. Passing from girlhood to womanhood is like the "frost that falls in March, before spring comes" This leap into spring for the woman is "anguish, is pain, is rounded knowledge, is continuance. For woman pain and continuance be one, and for men death and joy are one. And that is the mystery of creation". Here is a statement of primeval reality which still lives in the present day life. Sexual pleasure with Madeline elevates him to heights where he experiences the "still wonder"—"the wonder that makes the sun shine or the moon speak." The inner experience of Ramaswamy finds analogy in the processes of nature. This link between the inner and outer fills him with a sense of continuity. He says :

You know the world will be, for it is ; you know the banana ripens on the stem and the coconut falls on the fertile earth—that rivers flow, that the *parijata* blossoms, white and pink between leaves. And as the wind wave after wave of it, and mountains move, the wind stops and you settle into yourself ; and you hear it again...(p. 159).

The Serpent and the Rope takes up the east—west theme and explores the differences and similarities between the two. It has been pointed oüt that through there is much incompatibility between the two at the personal and social levels, there is an essential oneness at the religious-philosophical plane.[9] While Ramaswamy instinctively reacts to his environment and perceives the holiness, Madelaine rationalises and separates. To her, Benares is a place "of bits of floating human flesh and pyres of [the dead, and the Ganges water when chemically examined shows no bacteria" (p. 39). She is a world apart even from the young Sridhara who stood "absorbed and quiet" gathering the holiness of generations when little mother recited the *Annapurna Slokam*. Accepting the alien myths was difficult for her while it was not so for Ramaswamy. The Durance is as much capable of giving Ramaswamy his *linga* as the river at Belur "where the god's image comes floating down the river, the whole town hears the OM as though sounded on a conch, and men and priests go with fife and drum and palanquin to get him to his sanctuary" (p. 54). To Ramaswamy India represents truth. It is the place where time and space are annihilated. His Indianness had given him the "hunger for a wholeness" which effaces distinctions of race, caste and creed. Ramaswamy is the true representative of the archetypal man whose mind revels inwardly in Brahman whatever he might be doing :

Yogarato Vaa Bhogarato Vaa
Sangarato Vaa Sanggaviheenah
Yasya Brahmani Ramate Chittam
Nandati Nandati Nandatyeva.[10]

("Whether one is a yogi given to austere living, or a bhogi given to luxuries, whether one has renounced everything

and has taken to sanyas, or is still in family attachments,
he alone will be truly happy and will verily enjoy who is
ravelling inwardly in Brahman)."
Even while analysing the various religions of the world,
Ramaswamy's attempt is to reduce their ideologies to a
general fundamental principle. Maintaining the co-existence of good and evil and the simultaneous presence of
contradictions in man, he remarks : "There is always a
Karna and an Uttara in every battle, whether their names be
changed to Innocent III or Hughes de Noyers, Bishop of
Auxerre. ...It was the same battle between Pascal and
the Jesuit Fathers" (p. 181). He tells Madelaine, who is
afraid that he would make a Hindu out of her, that "The
gods were neither Hindu nor Greek, being creations of your
own mind they behaved as you made them—if Shiva was
what I wanted, Shiva himself would come to the Durance"
(p. 55). "This anthropocentricity is beyond Madelaine but
she is yet capable of responding to her environment with
pagan delight and mystic questioning in her own way.
Watching the distant shores of the Mediterranean, "the
cradle of civilisation," fundamental questions such as
"Who am I ?" and "What am I doing here ?" (p.38) are
raised in her mind. The vision of Demeter rising out of
the sea comes to her with the same freshness as when she
was originally conceived and the mystic links with nature
are established whereby the sea becomes suspicious and
the world bathed in simple delight. Madelaine, Ramaswamy and Sridhara are one on the philosophical plane.

It would be justified to conclude that Raja Rao's sensibility is the sensibility of those times when there was no
fragmentation. He experiences a healthy wholeness,
which arises out of "over-whelming sense of wonder and
mystery and above all humility in the presence of the
mystery."[11] The loss of ability to wonder and feel the
mystery has resulted in the strophied modern sensibility.
Through numerous stories from Indian mythology, history
and folklore Raja Rao strives to bring to life the cherished
values of the Indian tradition. He delves into the Indian
psyche and touches the chord of the "myth-epic tradition

of the rural India,"[12] the absence of which, according to Jayanta Mahapatra, is responsible for the failure of Indian writing in English. *The Serpent and the Rope* captures the culture of the essential Indian and also that of the archetypal man. It picks up the chain of this unique heritage and makes available to all readers the joys of contemplating. It would only be proper to conclude with Ramaswamy's words : "I felt as though at each epoch, with each person, I had left knowledge of myself, and in this affirmation of the presence that I am, I am my brother" (p. 128).

REFERENCES

1. See Northrop Frye, "Literary Criticism", *The Aims and Methods of Scholarship in Modern Languages and Literatures*, (ed.) James Thorpe (Hyderabad : American Studies Research Centre, 1970).
2. C.D. Narasimhaiah, *Raja Rao*, [New Delhi : Arnold-Heineman Publishers (India) Pvt. Ltd.], p. 74.
3. *Ibid.*, p. 80.
4. *Ibid.*, p. 80.
5. *Ibid.*, p. 80.
6. Raja Rao, *The Serpent and the Rope*, (Delhi : Orient Paperbacks, 1968), p. 36. All subsequent textual references, given parenthetically, are from this edition.
7. John B. Alphonso Karkala, "Myth, Matrix and Meaning in Literature and Raja Rao's Novel *Kenthapura*", *Perspective on Raja Rao*, (ed.) K.K. Sharma (Ghaziabad : Vimal Prakashan, 1980), p. 72.
8. Northrop Frye, *Languages of Criticism and the Structure of Poetry*.
9. O.P. Mathur, "The Serpent Vanishes : A Study in Raja Rao's Treatment of the East-West Theme." *Perspectives on Raja Rao* (ed.), Sharma, p. 45.
10. Sankara's Bhaja Govindam, Verse, 19.
11. Narasimhaiah, *Raja Rao*, p. 148.
12. Jayanta Mahapatra, "The Inaudible Resonance in English Poetry in India", *The Literary Criterion*, Vol. 15, 1980.

7

Khwaja Ahmad Abbas's The Naxalites : An Unusual Story of Unusual People

SUNIL KUMAR

K.A. Abbas, a noted journalist, is the author of over sixty fiction and non-fiction books, many of which have been best-sellers. Some of his better known works are : *That Woman, Outside India, Inquilab, Janta in a Jam,* and also an autobiography entitled *I am Not an Island.*

A typical controversy surrounds Abbas's status as a writer. Abbas is depicted as a propagandist, journalist, story-teller or an all-denying writer, etc. His novels such as *Inquilab* or *The Naxalites* have been labelled as 'mere journalese.' The journalists on the other hand say that K.A. Abbas is no journalist, he is merely a story writer. This wide diversity of the opinions is a consequence not only of the critics' wealth of imagination but also of the complexity of Abbas's work. Whether he himself encouraged this sort of discordant confusion of opinions and evaluations is yet to be ascertained but his status as a novelist is now widely accepted and, in fact, unrefutable.

The Naxalites is an authentic account of the exploits of Naxalites. These dare-devil revolutionaries are depicted as characters in a real human drama, the naxalite movement which directly or indirectly had kept the nation tense over the last decade or so. The story is, in fact, a series of episodes. Each episode is a close up of individuals providing the readers background and finer traits of their personalities.

Abbas uses impressionistic and symbolist techniques to depict the human psyche. Judged from the traditional standards, *The Naxalites* does not have a compact plot. There is no set description of characters as in the older novel, there is a shift from the external to the inner self of the various personages. In this stream of consciousness novel Abbas has made use of 'cinematic devices' as 'flash backs' 'cuttings', 'Montage', 'panorama', close ups extensively to show interrelation or association of ideas.[1]

The pavements of Calcutta, the lush-green paddy fields in the village around 'Naxalbari', the jungles on the border of Bengal and Bihar form the background to the scene of "grim, bloody dialogue between two inexorable forces— the arrogant force of 'law and order' at all cost, and the impatient batallions of instant revolutions."[2]

As it is not possible to examine each and every episode in this paper I have singled out the episode designated as 'The Man who lived in a Grave', keeping in view the title of this paper.

Amarkaal which means 'Long Live Famine' is an important but unusual character in this episode. Abbas portrays the character of Amarkaal in a manner that it not only creates a psychological interest but also expresses his point of view regarding the naxalite movement. It is through the subconsciousness of Amarkaal that he tries to trace the genesis of the naxalite movement in the Great Bengal Famine of 1942-43 when Amarkaal, like many other naxalites belonging to the younger generation, was a child.

Amarkaal belongs to the tribe of unusual characters in *The Naxalites*. In this unusual episode Abbas describes him as a youngman "who lives in a christian-grave in an old and now disused British cemetery off Park Circus in Calcutta".[3]

When asked why had his mother or father given him an unusual name, he replies" May be. . .because I was born in the years of the Great Famine, my parents did not want me to forget that time ".[4]

Amarkaal is portrayed as a neurotic character. Although he denies remembering anything about his mother and father, the memories haunted him. Were these stray thoughts, memories or drama he was not sure. He is hesitant to share them with a "stranger, however kind he might be"[5] because of the fear that he may be declared crazy. The word 'Ma' stuns him to the core and the sight of a hungry baby crying on the pavement is virtually like a "sting of memory in his heart."[6]

Abbas lucidly reveals in this episode what he is about by placing an emphasis "on exploration of the pre-speech levels of consciousness for the purposes, primarily, of revealing the psychic being of the characters."[7] He uses stream of consciousness medium with a definite purpose in mind.

Since Abbas strongly feels that the genesis of naxalite movement is deeply rooted in the great Bengal Famine of 1943, he goes about to explain this truth on the level of mind that is not expressed.

Abbas deftly presents this point of view through a character Ajoy Bose a journalist, who meets Amarkaal in the court room by chance. It will not be farfetched to say that Abbas the novelist in the guise of Ajoy Bose the journalist guides the reader. K.A. Abbas has surpassed other writers in delineation of unconscious particularly in the case of Amarkaal who is extraordinarily sensitive. It is through his psyche that Abbas is able to establish the connection between the naxalite movement and the Bengal Famine. In the episode Ajoy Bose and Amarkaal go to see a film screened as a part of festival of old films called 'Nostalgia'. About the film Abbas writes :

"But it was not a pleasant nostalgia—it revived memories of the Great Famine of Bengal of 1943 and recreated the atmosphere of those days, how one peasant family, driven by starvation, had to migrate to Calcutta, along with thousands of peasant families."[8]

The vivid scene of a long caravan of peasants flowing towards the city, and a child in rags, lost, looking about for his parents stimulates the subconscious part of Amarkaal's memory. He begins to identify himself with the characters in the scene to the extent that a dark little urchin or the crying baby on pavement appears to him as his own image. Ajoy Bose tries to intervene in the incoherent remarks (of Amarkaal). He says :

"Thats not your mother but a famous actress who, by her acting, is depicting what happened to your mother and thousands of other women during the famine :"[9]

In a violent reaction Amarkaal rushes towards the screen crying out for his mother. Immediately after this incident Ajoy Bose takes Amarkaal to a woman psychiatrist. On a couch under the influence of a sedative he responds like a child to the questions of the psychiatrist. She tells Ajoy Bose : "such cases are rare...he has mother fixation. The mother's lap was snatched from him in childhood since then he has been hankering for it."[10]

About the violent reaction while seeing the film she tells Bose that it is a psychological disease. Amarkaal's sub-conscious holds him responsible for his mother's down-fall and death. "Perhaps she was selling herself to bring milk for the baby."[11]

The entire conversation between psychiatrist and the journalist merits attention. I have singled out the following excerpt which expresses [the novelist's point of view sufficiently. When asked by the journalist about some cure for Amarkaal she says :

"The cure for him is to be helped and educated to identify the forces that were responsible for the Famine and for the death of his mother. His complex will go when he realizes that he himself is the victim of the same forces which caused his mother's death. The death has to be avenged !"

From a doctor, now she was talking like a revolutionary. Then again she became a woman, the universal mother :

"Tell me, child, from which village did your parents come to Calcutta ?"
From his semi-somnolence Amarkaal momentarily came out, as he replied :

"From Naxalbari !"

"Naxalbari ?". The psychiatrist repeated. "We have never heard the name of this village," said Ajoy Bose, "May be it is in Darjeeling district."

"I have been sleeping in a grave in Calcutta", replied Amarkaal, still not out of his daze, "But I want to go to Naxalbari."[12]

It becomes very clear to the reader now what Abbas the author has tried to establish through the psyche of the character. Once out of the nightmare Amarkaal is able to identify the forces responsible for the Famine and his mother's death. Amarkaal joins the ranks of Naxalites and even dies in an encounter with the police but not before he has avenged his mother's death by killing the 'Jothedar' of the village 'Naxalbari.'

Like Amarkaal, Kanu Santhal, Ajitha, Ashoke Mazumdar and Kamla Sen are all unusual people in the story. Each episode of the novel is a story of these unusual people, the naxalites. Abbas makes an honest probe into the psychology of certain human beings whose motto is "Khatam Kar do—ya khatam ho jao !"[13] For these people wedded to the concept of revolution no sacrifice seems to be great. Their enthusiasm and will is inexhaustible, prepared to be tortured or to torture others.

Abbas tries to draw the attention of the readers towards certain unresolved basic issues such as :

(a) Are the naxalites merely blood-thirsty revengeful souls, "common murderers" or dedicated victims who believe in the establishment of a new social order by wrestling the power through the barrel of gun ?

(b) How are naxalites born ? Will the use of brutal force by uniformed soldiers be able to exterminate them ?

The novel is full of ironical statements which raise these issues. Dr Ashraf Ali, a physician turned naxalite, for instance, was "today taking lives instead of saving lives."[15] In this fact-packed novel Abbas not only tries to trace the genesis of naxalite movement but also expresses his opinion regarding the futility of the methods adopted by the naxalites and the counter steps taken by the government.

In the last episode entitled 'Message from the Gallows ;' Ajitha the condemned naxalite manages to send a message to her comrades before she is hanged :

Comrades, think what you are doing—You have killed enough—and sufficient number of you have been killed. Some at hands of Naxalites. Think whether it has led us to the goal of revolution. Not murder; but mass awakening, mass organization, is the way to revolution. I am not afraid to die—you asked me to kill and I killed—even the one I loved ; you asked me to die and I am dying—but from the threshold of Death I am sending this message to you to reconsider your methods. . ."[16]

Interestingly, some of the names of these unusual people in the story have a note of familiarity. Kanu Santhal, Ashoke Mazumdar may remind the readers of Kanu Sanyal and Charu Mazumdar—the self-styled leaders of the naxalite movement.

Although *The Naxalites* may be an unusual story of unusual people, it successfully portrays reality. Abbas himself says about the novel : "All characters—and incidents—in this novel are fictitious, but none is entirely imaginary."[17]

REFERENCES

1. Robert Humphrey, *Stream of Consciousness in the Modern Novel*, Los Angeles : University of California Press, 1965, p. 49.
2. Khwaja Ahmad Abbas, *The Naxalites*, Delhi : Lok Publications, 1979, p. 16.
3. *Ibid.,* p. 15.
4. *Ibid.,* p. 15.
5. *Ibid.,* p. 16.
6. *Ibid.,* p. 22.
7. Humphrey, *Stream of Consciousness in the Modern Novel*, p. 4.
8. *The Naxalites*, p. 21.
9. *Ibid.,* p. 21.
10. *Ibid.,* p. 22.
11. *Ibid.,* p. 23.
12. *Ibid.,* pp. 23, 24.
13. *Ibid.,* p. 11 'Kill or be Killed.'
14. *Ibid.,* p. 110.
15. *Ibid.,* p. 12.
16. *Ibid.,* p. 110.
17. Abbas's declaration before the prologue.

8

Alienation in Kamala Markandaya's Some Inner Fury: A Study of Characters

C. SENGUPTA

One of the major by-products of the industrial civilisation is a sense of alienation that it has given to humanity at large. Today, alienation as a concept has taken deep roots in everyday life, in science, in philosophy, in psychology, sociology and literature — covering a large gamut of almost every aspect of man's activity. Most of the definitions of alienations are modifications of one broad meaning which is suggested by the etymology of the word itself. Alienation (or estrangement) is the act, or the result of the act, through which something or somebody, becomes alien, or strange (r) to some thing or somebody else.[1]

In common usage, alienation stands for a turning away or keeping away from those who were hitherto friends or associates. In modern arts and literature, it is often used to denote an individual's feeling of alienness toward society, nature, other people or himself.[2] For many writers alienation is a synonym for reification : "the act, or the result of the act, of transferring human properties, relations and actions into properties and actions of things which are independent of man and which govern his life".[3] To certain other writers alienation stands for "self-alienation (self-estrangement)'' : a process or the result of a process, through which a 'self', that is, God or man, through itself, that is, through its own action, becomes alien or strange to itself, that is, to its own nature.

There is a wide ranging diversity in the understanding and use of the term ''alienation''. A few believe that the term can be applied both to man and to non-human objects (to God, world, nature, for example) ; but a large number insists that the term is applicable only to man. Some among the latter, insist that it can be correctly applied only to individuals and not to society at large. According to a good number of such authors, alienation is signalled by the non-adjustment of an individual to the society in which he lives. There are still others, who contend that a society also can be alienated or ''sick'', so that the non-adjustment of an individual to his society need not necessarily be a sign of that individual's alienation.

Alienation has assumed the proportions of a great problem in modern fiction, whether British, American or Indo-Anglian. This paper is an attempt to analyse the theme of alienation in Kamala Markandaya's Some Inner Fury through an in-depth analysis of the characters.

II

In Some Inner Fury the theme of alienation is brought out very well through the juxtaposition of the opposite traits in Kitsamy and Govind. Kitsamy is totally alienated from the Indian way of life. His whole attitude to life is Anglicised (he has just returned from Oxford) and the discerning reader notices the little nuances : he goes out with Richard Marlowe (his Oxford friend) in all his finery, asks for a glass of beer and points out that Richard, being a foreigner, is affected by flowering trees like gulmohur.[4] Kit's mother succinctly remarks : ''poor Kitsamy, he feels the heat. He will have to make a lot of adjustments''[5]

Govind (Kit's adopted brother), on the other hand, is very much steeped in Indian culture but is an alien in the society in which Kit moves. The difference between Kit and Govind is skilfully revealed in their attitude towards the ubiquitous Dodamma:

> Then Kit started complaining about the toothless old woman Dodamma—she's everywhere, you can't help bumping into her, must she be so evident? And what he meant was that he found her, perhaps vicariously, unlovely and embarrassing as she went about—as a widow should—with short head and wearing no blouse under her sari, as you sometimes saw when the cloth slipped from her shoulders ..... Govind, unexpectedly vocal, aligned himself with Dodamma : why should she, his own kith-and-kin, put herself out for this Englishman ?[6]

Thus, as R.S. Pathak points out, "Kit is a typical alienated person, who is only a vine clinging to the British Raj, having no individual identity of his own".[7] Kit's alienation goes rather deep. It would seem that he has imbibed only the superficial aspects of Western culture. His household is modelled and run in perfectly English Style, 'there being nothing that was Indian about it'.[8] Unfortunately, his wife Premala who is deeply embedded in the traditional Indian way of life, hates going to clubs and leading the kind of social life that Kit enjoys. It is natural that Govind, with his roots firmly in the native soil, should fall in love with Premala. And given Premala's total identification with Indian mores, it is natural that Govind's love for Premala will go unrequited.

Though Govind is very much a son of the soil, in a sense he is also alienated and rootless. In Kit's family he is an outsider, being Kit's adopted brother, and the attitude of both Kit and his parents to Govind is one of condescension. It is only Mira and later Premala who really understand him. Kit's condescension towards Govind very often verges on the insult. The images associated with Govind are dark and silent and the scene where Kit and Govind confront each other over the issue of feeding the urchins in festivities preceding Kit's marriage to Premala. The novelist fuses the images of light and dark, which effectively reveals the antagonism between the two:

The two men confronted each other : Kit, bright with anger, its banners vivid and flaring in his cheeks; Govind, dark and smoldering, the blood slowly ebbing from his face and leaving it the colour of ashes.[9]

Thus there seems to be a fire smouldering in Govind, the fire of revolt because he has been denied true affection and, like a volcano seething with hidden lava, it finds an outlet in revolutionary activities. Thus the conflict between Kit and Govind is not only a conflict between two natures vastly different, it is also a conflict between native and alien mores : Kit is as much rootless as Govind is. Kit seems to be what Kamala Markandaya in a later novel calls 'Nowhere man', neither truly Indian, nor truly English. And Govind, though a product of traditional Indian way of life is alienated from his immediate environment because he has chosen a life of violence and destruction. Just as Govind is an 'outsider' in the family circle of Kit and Mirabai and their parents, Kit appears as an outsider in the domestic scene when Govind pays a visit to Premala, now Kit's wife :

Govind, link with a life she loved and understood ......
And he responded as he has always done, speaking as no one but she could make him, rapidly and without restraint.[10]

But as Kit's footsteps are heard,

Already, though Kit was not yet in the room, the atmosphere was changing; shifting, dissolving, surrendering its glow, taking on neutrality as if preparing for something *alien* to be introduced into it.[11]

III

A careful reading of the novel, *Some Inner Fury*, will show Premala also suffering from an identity crisis. With her gentle, unpretentious ways, and her deep disgust for tennis and club-going and (later when married) almost daily social rounds, she is a misfit in Kit's life. But the spark of rebellion in Premala is not dead and so she drifts away from Kit and finds fulfilment in her adopted daughter and her school. As a character, she grows and changes.

When she sees that she cannot fit into Kit's world with its almost daily round of parties and dances, she builds a world of her own and lives there, if not totally contented, partly. As the novelist puts it succinctly : "Indeed it (the school) was becoming her world, for she could find no place in the one her husband inhabited."[12] Her involvement with the school is total (just as Govind's involvement with the freedom movement is complete) and is revealed in the way taking fright at Govind's warning she dashes to the villages to save the school at a tremendous risk to herself. Thus in the ultimate analysis Premala and Govind are kindred spirits.

In the initial stages of the novel Roshan has been delineated as a sophisticated product of western culture 'in a chiffon sari coloured like a rainbow, and slippers with rhinestone heels, and a mouth as bright and vivid as a geranium petal'.[13]

But these are only superficial trappings and when the crunch comes she identifies herself totally with India's freedom movement. After showing Kit as thoroughly Westernized, Kamala Markandaya restores the balance in the portrayal of Roshan Merchant. Though a streak of flippancy always remains with her, she bridges the gulf between the East and the West and shines as a splendid synthesis of the two opposite cultures. As Kamala Markandaya points out through Mira :

> It was Roshan who came nearest to him (Richard Marlowe) in liking sympathy for the ways of the West; but she belonged to the East too. Born in one world, educated in another, she entered both and moved in both with ease and nonchalant. It was a dual citizenship which few people had, which a few may have spurned, but many more envied and which she herself simply took for granted.[14]

Slowly but surely the novelist shows the change that overtakes Roshan :

> Roshan went her way unperturbed, bright and fearless as she had always been, Under Govind's tutelege she began and kept up, which was more than many people

did—a boycott of British goods. She stopped smoking ; she gave up, regretfully, using lip-stick. . . . there was the time she sorted out all her British manufactured georgette and chiffon saries and repaired with them to the maidan where she threw them on the bonfire which other women of her convictions had kindled and were feeding with similar fuel—thereafter wearing. . . the pre- scribed rough homespun. . . .There was something in her, a flame, a vitality, which drew people to her despite themselves ; and this quality, which she possessed so lightly as hardly to be aware of it, enabled her to sur- mount the barriers not only of race and creed but also — perhaps even more formidable—that of politics.[15]

IV

An analysis of the character of Richard Marlowe and that of the narrator Mirabai shows that though both of them have achieved a mature balance between two cultures—East and West, when the crunch comes Mira displays her allegiance to the freedom movement and *her* own people, whereas Richard remains with *his* people. Thus both suffer an identity crisis at the end and the final choice is tragic for both.

In the early pages of the novel, Richard emerges as a contrast to Kit willing to adopt himself to the alien environ- ment without discarding the rich sensibility of his own culture. He has imbibed the Indian way of life as natu- rally as a duck takes to water, and as Mira's lover, he dis- plays a fine balance of passion and restraint. But when they come back from their 'honeymoon' and the 'Quit India' movement is at its peak and has assumed violent propor- tions Richard realizes that even though he has tried his best to imbibe Indian way of life, as the Governor's A.D.C. he is still an outsider. The novelist is quite explicit about Richard's sentiments here :

He (Richard) looked at me with level eyes. He said, "It's a terrible thing to feel unwanted. To be hated."[16]

Mirabai, the centre of consciousness in the novel, is delineated with loving care. She is the author's voice and seems to share many of her traits. A heightened sensibility and imaginative vigour have settled at the very core of her personality. Though she is brought up in a tradition-al household, she rises above the outward trappings of tradition and identifies herself with all that is good in Western culture without giving up her roots. Her feet are firmly planted in the native soil. It is natural that such a charac-ter that has achieved a judicious synthesis between Wes-tern and Indian ways of life will be attracted to a kindred spirit, Richard Marlowe, who is the very apotheosis of this synthesis. It is only at the latter pages of the novel that Mira suffers a feeling of alienation from Richard and his people, which the author brings out very well in the follo-wing, almost incoherent, utterance :

> "Richard—this feeling isn't for you. Or—or for people like you. You must believe me....I would not lie to you."[17]

Thus the identity crisis in Mira takes the form of the choices that she makes at the end of the novel. The first choice is her determination to defend Govind ; to declare in the court that Govind could not have killed Kit because she had his (Govind's) arms pinioned. The second choice that she makes is to throw her lot with the freedom move-ment and thereby abandon Richard. Kamala Markandaya's first person narration puts this choice in perspective thus :

> Go ? Leave the man I loved to go with these people ? What did they mean to me, what could they mean, more than the man I loved ? They were *my* people—those others were *his*. Did it mean something then—all this "your people" and "my people" ? Or did it have its being and gain its strength from ceaseless repetition ? They are nothing to you, cried my heart. Nothing, nothing. If you go now, there will be no meaning in anything evermore. But that stark illuminated moment— of madness, of sanity—went, and I knew I would follow these people even as I knew Richard must stay. For us there was no other way, the forces that pulled as apart were too strong.[18]

Thus when the crunch comes, when she has to make an irrevocable decision, she decides in favour of the 'forces' of nationalism and her identity crisis, her feeling of aliena-tion is resolved.

REFERENCES

1. G. Petrovies, "Alienation" *Encyclopedia of Philosophy* Vol. I ed. Paul Edwards (New York : Macmillan, 1972).
2. *Ibid.*
3. *Ibid.*
4. *Some Inner Fury* (New York ; The John Day Company, 1956), p. 18.
5. *Ibid.*, p. 13.
6. "The Alienated Protagonist in the Indo-English Novel", in *Glimpses of Indo-English Fiction* ed. O.P. Saxena (New Delhi : Jainsons Publication, 1985), p. 78.
7. *Some Inner Fury*, p. 83.
8. *Ibid.*, pp. 58-59.
9. *Ibid.*, p. 102.
10. *Ibid.*, p. 103.
11. *Ibid.*, p. 141.
12. *Ibid.*, p. 12.
13. *Ibid.*, p. 28.
14. *Ibid.*, pp. 155-56.
15. *Ibid.*, p. 195.
16. *Ibid.*
17. *Ibid.*, p. 253.

9

East-west Encounter in Jhabvala's Esmond in India

(Miss) MRIDULA BAJPAI

Ruth Prawer Jhabvala is one of the outstanding Indo-English women novelists. Her novels deal with post-Independence India. While she was living in Delhi with her Indian husband, Mrs Jhabvala had many opportunities of observing Indians and also foreigners who came to India, at close quarters. She concentrates on European expatriates and the members of the educated Hindu middle-class families. The major themes of her novels are love, marriage and familial relationships.

In Mrs Jhabvala's novels, India reacts strongly on her Western characters and transforms them to a large extent. She skillfully describes the experiences of Westerners in India and their interaction with Indians. Her foreignness enables her to deal with mixed marriages of Indians and Europeans in a critical but amused manner. The differences in their life-styles and religions are vividly presented. In fact, the interaction between the two cultures, Eastern and Western, forms an integral part of her novels.

Esmond in India and *A Backward Place* present the experiences of an Indian woman married to a European and a European woman married to an Indian. India, chiefly because of her ancient culture, attracts many Europeans. Some of them, like Esmond and Judy in *Esmond in India* and *A Backward Place* respectively, fall in love with Indian culture and life, and want to settle down here. They marry Indians. But the marriage between East and West does not result in harmony. European husbands and Indian wives or Indian husbands and European wives are unable to maintain a co-existence without a clash of personalities.

In *Esmond in India* Gulab marries an Englishman named Esmond Stillwood. But their relationship is not peaceful. The differences in the life-styles of East and West lead to misunderstanding and discord. Consequently their relations are strained and they drift apart.

Esmond Stillwood is an impoverished expatriate, who earns his living by giving private tutions to foreign ladies, tourists and Indian elite. He teaches them "Hindustani or the History of Indian Art or the History of Indian Literature" (p. 42).[1] An Englishman tells Shakuntala that Esmond has "come specially to India to teach you people all about your own country" (p. 81). Gulab is so charmed by his speeches that she rejects the eligible Amrit and marries Esmond against the wishes of her mother, Uma.

The novelist depicts very convincingly Gulab's Indian tastes and habits and how they are resented by the very English Esmond. Gulab is lazy and when Esmond is not at home "she would stay on her bed for hours and hours" (p. 16). Esmond hates her laziness. He screams at her and asks : "What sort of a slut's life is that to lie on your bed the whole day long ?" (p. 202). Their eating habits are vastly different. Gulab loves eating sweets and oily food. She dwells on the possibility "of eating food from her mother's house" (p. 18). On Wednesdays and Fridays, she is very happy because Esmond has early morning classes and her mother brings something to eat. She wonders : "When would Esmond be away from home during the day and for how long" (p. 17). She likes to spend time with her mother, but Esmond fails to understand the overdependence of an Indian girl on her mother for guidance in all matters. He feels left out and neglected.

The married life of Esmond and Gulab deteriorates after the birth of a son, Ravi. Esmond wants to bring up the child in the European way and keep him away from Indian food. He dislikes Gulab for not paying proper attention to Ravi's food habits. He fails to understand his mother-in-law when she suggests to :

> have his (Ravi) legs rubbed with oil to make him strong and his hair must be shaved so that it may grow luxuriant, and black shadows must be applied under his eyes to shield them from strong sun, and in the night he must sleep with his mother so that she may comfort him if he wakes with bad dreams (p. 142).

Esmond gets angry when Gulab applies Indian scent to Ravi. He detects the smell and says : "Why don't you throw the horrible stuff away ?" (p. 44). He feels that she is spoiling the child with caresses and sweets. In Esmond's absence, Gulab kisses Ravi and calls him "My soul, ... My life, my little tiny sweetmeat" who himself "would kiss her back again ardently" (p. 17).

Gulab stays at home with her son and does not accompany Esmond anywhere. She reverts to Indian ways in his absence. He asks and checks about Ravi's food when he comes back. The servants also have contempt for Esmond's food. They say he 'eats grass for his food' (p. 23). He decorates his flat and the furniture is modern but Gulab finds it a hinderance. He is very particular about keeping the house clean and dislikes Gulab's untidiness. Mrs Jhabvala describes the cultural clash between East and West skillfully and in detail. Esmond and Gulab are brought into very close association with a view to highlighting the difference between them. Although a lover of Indian culture and life, he is unable to understand it completely and cope with its oddities.

Esmond can no longer take any delight in Gulab's 'Indian English' (p. 47). He reprimands her: "I don't mind...what sort of babu English you choose to speak—I couldn't, as they say, be careless—but that you might infect the boy with it too, that's what bothers me" (p. 48). To his great annoyance, his sarcasm is lost on her when he shouts and asks : "If pressed to the point would you call yourself a slut ?" (p. 47). She does not understand the connotations of his language.

The novelist describes the annoyance of Esmond at his Indian wife. Indian ways and life are totally lost on him. Sarcastically he calls Gulab a 'Model little wife' (p. 48). The novelist writes of him :

> He thought of himself as trapped—trapped in her stupidity, in her dull heavy alien mind which could understand nothing, neither him, nor his way of life nor his way of thought (p. 46).

Esmond says of his marriage that 'Every man has his cross' and finds that 'his was heavier than that of other men' (p. 46).

Gulab shows no response to Esmond's taunts. When Shakuntala visits their house, she finds that Gulab neither drinks nor smokes. Esmond sarcastically remarks; "I' ve tried so hard to corrupt her...but her virtues are too deep-rooted for my little arts" (p. 127). Esmond also points out that Ravi has taken after him 'only in complexion' (p. 127). Esmond finds himself neglected by his wife and begins fo drift towards Betty who was "so light, and modern and airy. Being with her was almost as good as being in England, which was the one place where he wanted most passionately to be" (p. 49).

Gulab has her happy moments whe she gets the opportunity of escaping to her mother's house. She disobeys Esmond's orders and visits her mother. "She did not want anything to spoil her stay with her mother" (p. 163). When she is at home; she tulerates Esmond's taunts, infidelities and cruelities. She behaves in a traditional Indian role of a meek wife. She believes that :

> She must, whatever he might do to her, stay with Esmond, since he was her husband and therefore her God...It was a husband's right, so her instinct told her, to do whatever he liked with his wife. He could treat her well or badly, pamper her or beat her—that was upto him, and it was not her place to complain (P. 248).

Mrs Jhabvala takes an opportunity to comment on marriages and the eastern concept of marriage. Married life is full of problems, as is evident from the cases of Ram Nath and Lakshmi. In the relationship of Har Dayal and Madhuri also, who have been happily married for long, we perceive an emptiness. Madhuri's consolation comes from her son Amrit, who is a 'good sensible boy' (p. 91). All her life she has 'put up with an unstable husband' (p. 91) Elder couples, even when they feel trapped together, are unable to break away from an unsatisfactory relationship. Gulab's case is strange. She marries Esmond against the wishes of her mother and bears him a son. She stands his insolence, sarcasm and beating to the extent that he even calls her 'animal' (p. 204). All along she is shown as a weak and lazy woman who is always eating and sleeping. Her mother repeatedly tells her to leave Esmond and return home, which she refuses to do. But when the servant tries to molest her, with an innate strength she decides to return to her mother's house with Ravi, for as a husband Esmond fails in his duty :

> It was his duty to see that she was safe in his house and that no stranger could cast insulting eyes on her. Esmond had failed in that duty; so now he was no more her husband. Nor she is his wife, and since she considered herself defiled, she could not remain in his house any longer but had to return, as was the custom, to her own people (p. 248).

She does not even care to shut the door of the flat.

Shakuntala, a romantic straight out of college, throws herself into the arms of Esmond, the 'Don Juan'. Fed on Byron and Shelley, she is in love with the idea of freedom. When she sees Esmond, she is attracted to him. "She decided at once that he was, yes, very handsome. Much more so than any of the other foreigners there. He was slim and graceful, and while they were red and rather raw, he was pale, with golden hair and a fine pointed chin. He looked so sensitive, she thought, like a poet" (p. 80). What makes her so deeply interested in Esmond is the fact that he is the "Englishman who had come so suddenly and taken Gulab away from Amrit" (p. 80). Har

Dayal engages Esmond to teach her all about the cultural aspects of East and West. She sees his unhappy married life and feels sorry for him. She wonders "why did he marry her [Gulab]" (p. 128). While on a trip to Taj Mahal seduces Shakuntala in his hotel bedroom.

Iyengar writes that in Mrs Jhabvala's novels the focus is on a 'trapped married couple'[2] In *Esmond in India*, Gulab and Esmond are the unhappy couple. They fail to come to a better understanding. Gulab does not understand him when he says." I want a wife who's my friend and companion, not my slave" (p. 205). But he also has Betty in mind when he tells Gulab : "I regard my wife as an equal and I expect her to regard her as such" (p. 205). He fails to get any response from her whether his behaviour is good or bad towards her. People belonging to widely different backgrounds, races and cultures face problems in adjusting themselves with each other. They do not even find a common point of discussion. Esmond feels that their relationship has reached a stage where there is no chance of any happiness. He compares his predicament with that of his friends and finds his state worse than theirs :

> There were, he knew, many other incompatible marriages; he had much experience of them among his friends. But there was always some neutral ground on which the two parties could meet. They could, occasionally and in between their quarrels, converse about indifferent subjects, if not like friends then at least like strangers shut up together in a railway compartment or they could sit and discuss their incompatability and so get some satisfaction out of rationalising their unhappiness (p. 206).

The novelist describes in detail the mental make-up of eastern women, who tolerate any kind of treatment which their husband meet out to them. Ram Nath describes their condition to Uma as follows :

> So like animals, like cows......Beat them, starve them, maltreat them how you like, they will sit and look with animal eyes and never raise a hand to defend themselves, saying "do with me what you will, you are my husband, my God, it is my duty to submit to my God" (p. 97).

Although married life is full of problems, there are parents in the novel who are busy in wife-hunting or husband-hunting the traditional method of arranging marriage after taking into consideration caste, family, status, future prospects, wealth, and so on. Shakuntala receives two very good offers of marriage from Professor Bhatnagar's son and from Ram Nath's son. But she is infatuated with Esmond. The younger generation do not favour an arranged marriage.

Ram Nath fully understands Gulab's unhappiness. He analyses precisely the marital dissonance in a mixed marriage. He tells her to leave her husband because she is unable to achieve any happiness from such a relationship:

> He [Esmond] is a very different person from you and he does not understand you and the way you live and think, the way we all live and think. I think he should not be in this country at all because he in no way belongs here, but I do not want to speak about that. All I want to speak about is that it is wrong for you to stay with him. It happens very often that there are differences between husband and wife, that they quarrel and do not agree. When these differences go very deep, it is better for husband and wife to part, because otherwise they will begin to hate one another and that is very ugly (p. 164).

The impact of India on foreigners is very strong. Initially, they love rich Indian art and culture. But after living through 'eternal shabbiness wrapped in eternal heat' (p. 252), they are transformed. Ruth Jhabvala in an autobiographical essay admits :

> I have lived in India for most of my life. My husband is Indian and so are my children. I am not, and less so every year.[3]

Esmond, who once found Gulab's eyes 'full of all wisdom and the sorrow of East'. found them 'a mere blank' (p. 206). The Indian experience transforms him completely. He is surprised at the transformation but accepts it. 'There was no romance about life in India, Esmond knew : only for tourists, he bitterly thought, who clapped their hands in delight over what was, he knew only shabbiness and poverty repeated to a point where the spirit yawned at the boredom and futility of it all" (p. 252).

Writing of Jhabvala's western characters, Meenakshi Mukherjee remarks that she sends them "back to Europe and America where they would once again live within their own family limits"[4]. Towards the end of Mrs Jhabvala's novel, the English seem to be packing their bags and preparing to return to England. Esmond plans to return along with Betty. He cannot carry on with an unhappy marriage with Gulab. He is disgusted with her; "His senses revolted at the thought of her, of her greed and smell and langour, her passion for meat and for spices and strong perfumes" (p. 207). Esmond also does not want to act as Shakuntala's lover. 'Gulab behind him and Shakuntala before him, but all he wanted was to be free' (p. 250).

Esmond decides to get away from Shakuntala and Gulab (not knowing that she has already left him), from India's shabbiness and poverty and from young ladies and cultural sessions. He makes arrangements to sail on the same boat as Betty, responding to her call to 'Pack up and come along' (p. 252). He imagines himself enjoying life in her company on the ship. He thinks; "Everything would be left behind and would be happy all day long and light hearted" (p. 253). He discovers that 'life was beginning for him again, he was young yet, young' (p. 253).

The two major female characters of the novel, Shakuntala and Gulab, thus achieve nothing substantial out of their relationship with Esmond. Gulab, who is Esmond's wife, allows him to illtreat her because he is her 'God'. She makes nothing of Ram Nath's advice to her that "No person has a right to treat another person in any fashion he likes. Please remember you are an individual being first and a wife only second" (p. 165). However, she is fortunate enough to have reached a decision on her own to leave Esmond. Shakuntala in her infatuation begs Esmond to allow her to be his slave. She is so blinded by her love for him that she is unable to see her plight. There can be no future for her with a cad like Esmond. By seducing her, he awakens her to love. But he does not wish to have a long love affair with her. He finds himself 'trapped in her love for him' (p. 233). He tries to extricate himself slowly by telling her "Your father has called me here because he trusted me, and whatever my feelings for you might be, I have to suppress them as long as I 'm in his house" (p. 233). No one can help her. She herself will have to work out her salvation because Esmond is ready to abandon her.

As Haydn Moore Williams observes, "By the end of the novel some of the characters—the simple and the idealist —have found a kind of peace : Gulab, Uma, Ram Nath. It is the sophisticated, the highly intelligent, the ambitious, the materialistic, who are fundamentally the lost and the unhappy of Jhabvala's world".[5] Shakuntala will have to set right her broken life. Iyengar aptly sums up the issues raised by Mrs Jhabvala in this novel : "The pathetic rootlessness of the foreigner in India and the tragicomic rootlessness of the Indian who has become westernized to feel at home with his own people".[6] Esmond and Shakuntala are the examples. Esmond's love for India is mercenary and Shakuntala's love for Esmond is sentimental.

Various experiences of Indian cultural scene are projected through the attitudes and gestures of Mrs Jhabvala's Western and Indian characters. Her India is moulded by the experiences of the protagonists. The interaction between two cultures, Indian and European, forms an essential part of her novels. She portrays the clash between East and West very convincingly. Being originally a European and later living in India, her country by adoption, she is able to create necessary background to treat the problems of Europeans trying to get adjusted to Indian society. They are unable to come to terms with the Indian ways and customs. They are disillusioned and the Indian sky remains "an unchanging unending expanse of white-blue glare, the epitome of meaningless monotony which dwarfed all human life into insignificance" (p. 252). Once they decide to return, they feel happy and relieved.

Ruth Jhabvala probes the mind and heart of her characters trapped in an unhappy marriage. The focus is on a mixed marriage. An European like Esmond Stillwood, who loves India and wants to settle down here and has an Indian wife, is unable to develop a lasting love for India. He remains rootless here. The East and West meet, but cannot integrate and blend. Although educated Indian girls like Gulab may be attracted towards a foreigner and even marry him, the relationship has an emptiness. They fail to understand each other's different life-styles. After the initial attraction fades, there is no common ground for interaction left. Gulab always desires that Esmond should be away from home so that she can live the way she wants. And Esmond finds himself trapped with her in the "flat which he had tried to make so elegant and charming, but which she had managed to fill completely with her animal presence" (p. 207).

The East and the West attract each other and will continue to do so because of their diverse characteristics. Despite the unhappy experiences of Esmond and Gulab, Har Dayal's younger son, Raj has acquired an English fiance. In a close encounter, as in the case of Esmond and Gulab, the East and West once again betray their incompatability. The differences of manners, customs, attitudes and modes of living result in discord and confusion. While delineating the confrontation between alien and the native with each other, the novelist focusses our attention on married couples who ultimately decide to live separately. If a man wants to be free and happy, it can also be a woman's prerogative. Throughout the novel Esmond feels trapped in an unhappy relationship. In the end he decides to be free and so does Gulab.

The East-West marriage is not the only unhappy marriage in the novel. Married life does not take a smooth course for anyone. All the married couples have their disappointments and unfulfilled desires. There is a lack of understanding and a communication gap between Indian husbands and their wives also. But Mrs Jhabvala draws our special attention to problems of the couples united in a mixed marriage. They face greater difficulty in adjusting themselves because of their diverse backgrounds and life-styles. They do not take adequate steps to come to an agreement and are continually put off by each other's drawbacks and different ways of eating, talking, dressing and so on. As a result, once the initial attraction is lost, there is no common ground left for interaction. The different characteristics which attract the East and the West, become so intolerable that they are unable to survive together.

REFERENCES

1. All textual references, given in parentheses are, from Ruth Prawer Jhabvala's *Esmond in India* (London : George Allen and Unwin Ltd., 1958).
2. K.R.S. Iyengar, *Indian Writing in English* (New Deihi : Asia Publishing House, 1973), p. 455.
3. Ruth Prawer Jhabvala, "Living in India", *London Magazine* (September 1970), p. 41.
4. Meenakshi Mukherjee, "Journey's End for Jhabvala", *Language Forum* (April 1981—March 1982), p. 211.
5. Haydn Moore Williams, *The Fiction of Ruth Prawer Jhabvala* (Calcutta : Writers Woskshop, 1973), p. 33.
6. Iyengar, *op. cit.*, 460.

10

Social and Political Scene in Nayantara Sahgal's earlier Novels

(Mrs) URMILA VARMA

Nayantara Sahgal is one of the prominent novelists of India, who recreates the Indian social and political scene just before and after the Independence in her writings. She is constantly concerned with men and women engaged in contemporary political life and ably describes, interprets and analyses the forces which determine human destiny. Political milieu is the dominent setting in her writings and if one considers the themes alone, her novels can be called political novels, but they are more than mere records of political events.

Her first novel. *A Time To Be Happy* (1955), is the story of Sanad against the backdrop of India's struggle for independence. It covers the period between 1932 to 1948 and narrates the story of Indian National Movement and its impact on the growing and young minds of the upper-middle class Indians. It also mirrors the smug attitude of the British and Indian Officers and their wives and focusses attention on the Indo-British relations as well. The locale of the novel is Saharanpur, a small town in Northern India having textile industry, mostly owned by the British and a couple of rich Indian businessmen. The story sometimes shifts to places such as Lucknow, Delhi and Calcutta, but it is Saharanpur which upholds the typical values, attitudes, traditions and culture of Northern India. It also brings out the superficial imposition of English culture on Indian people.

The story is narrated through the omniscient observer, who is a middle-aged bachelor. The novel unfolds the consciousness of Sanad, the main character, and his search for identity. The narrator believes in Gandhian ideology and he influences Sanad. The narrator's idealism and integrity is the source of strength for Sanad during all crucial moments. Being Westernised, Sanad feels alienated among Indians and ill at ease among the British officers of his company. Kusum Sahai's flair for Hindi and inclination for traditional Indian culture attracts him. They get married in 1947, the year of India's independence. Kusum feels uncertain about her marital relationship with Sanad, because she feels that he is living in an unreal and make-believe world of Anglo-Indians. Sanad's desire to attain Indianness is an interesting culmination of the novel.

Nayantara Sahgal has successfully captured the Anglo-Indian social attitudes and their false sense of racial pride. The Granges, the Weatherby, Trent and Marion remain aloof and arrogant. They are also unconcerned with the country's problems. Sanad reacts strongly to them and the anglicised Indians such as his uncle Harish, his brother Girish, the Chatterjis, Harilal Mathur and Vir Das.

Nineteen forty seven, the year of India's independence, triggers of a number of changes on the social and political fronts. Through the consciousness of her characters, Nayantara Sahgal has successfully captured the fragmentation of Indian psyche at that time. The abolition of Zamindari system disturbs Sanad's father, Govind Narayan. Among the other characters, Kunti Behen gets involved in new politics of elections, while Maya gets involved in rehabilitation of refugees. Only Sanad takes the changes on the social and political scene in stride but Kusum is emotionally affected by the violent and meaningless death of her brother Sahdev. The anglicised characters such as Girish feel lost in the new set-up. The Anglo-Indian business tycoons are also affected by the new changes.

Thematically, the novel operates on many levels. It depicts the upper-middle class consciousness of the Indian families. It portrays the superior and snobbish attitude of ruling class through the consciousness of Anglo-Indians and Anglicised Indians. Lastly, it shows the all-pervading impact of freedom movement under the leadership of Gandhi. It is not surprising that the women characters such as Maya, Lakshmi and Kusum represent the Indian culture. The novel depicts the slow and imperceptable changes on the Indian political and social scene, the intensification of the congress movement, the increasing industrialization, the changing social customs and manners. We become aware of the upper middle class Indians' rootlessness and the sense of not belonging to any of the two worlds—the slowly dying world of colonial values and the other of gradually emerging Indian identity. In this context, Sanad's desire to discover his own country is quite significant.[1]

Her second novel, *This Time of Morning* (1965), depicts the corrupt socio-political state of affairs after Independence. Its fictional world is peopled by a new breed of politicians of all sorts: bureaucrats, artists, journalists, parliamentarians, liberated ladies and housewives. It encompasses the elite of Delhi, which happens to be the nerve centre of power. Kalyan Sinha, the minister without portfolio, has lot of faith in group effort. Kailas, a Gandhian freedom fighter, however, thinks otherwise and believes in individual's capabilities. He has a magnetic personality and is "ruthlessly efficient". His identity is unknown, but the anonimity itself is the very source of his strength. During the course of the novel, Kalyan finally gains personal salvation, although he losses political power. It is through the love of Nita that he discovers himself and finds a home in her love. Kailas and Kalyan are opposites. Kailas believes that the corrupt framework of democracy can be redeemed by the Gandhian path of love of humanity, whereas Kalyan has a sort of contempt for individual human being. As a matter of fact, Rakesh is the central consciousness of the story of *This Time of Morning*. When the novel opens Rakesh is going through the state of uncertainity and anxiety. To begin with, Rakesh is uncommunicative.

According to him, it is only in an atmosphere of freedom that the state of dialogue is possible. Later, Rakesh finds solution to his personal as well as political problems through discussion. He says, "Discussion always serves a purpose"[2]. Thus the novel, besides being a record of socio-political scene of Delhi, shows Nayantara's basic concern with human values. Freedom in all spheres, according to her, is the prerequisite of all human progress.

Storm in Chandigarh (1969) describes the political turbulence in Punjab after 1947. The novel centres around the theme of forced linguistic bifurcation of the Punjab twenty years after its first post-independence communalistic partition. It shows the clash between Gyan Singh, the militant Chief Minister of Punjab and Harpal Singh, the Chief Minister of Haryana, Chandigarh, the joint capital of the Hindi-speaking Haryana and the Punjabi-speaking Punjab is the scene of action. Vishal Dubey is the young intellectual and an Indian Administrative officer who has been assigned the task of bringing out an accord between the two warring factions and to restore peace and harmony among the people of Chandigarh. The Union Home Minister's statement that "Violence lies very close to the surface in the Punjab"[3] is rather significant and reflects the situation that existed.

The fight between Gyan Singh and Harpal Singh is a fight of ideologies. It is a clash between the cult of violence and the ideal of non-violence. Nayantara brings out the evils of hypocrisy, pretence and snobbery existing at the human level, On the domestic front, violence emerges in the shape of male dominance in the marital relationship of Saroj and Inder. Vishal Dubey shows the way to Saroj to opt for a life without pretence. He is an advocate of the freedom of human spirit in all respects. The novel affirms the endless possibilities in human life both at political as well as inter-personal level. Nayantara's primary and serious concern is the confrontation of human spirit in a changing cultural milieu. Digging deeper in to the socio-political scene, one can see her characters struggling to find their roots.

Her next novel, *The Day in Shadow* (1971), begins where *Storm in Chandigarh* ends. The title of the novel refers to the violence after India's independence. It picks up the lives of people of Delhi, who are engaged in politics, business, and intellectual pursuits. These people include bureaucrates, freelance journalists and liberal thinkers. The crises that arise at this time of history are both personal as well as national. At the personal level, the crisis revolves around the married life of a free lance writer, Simrit, which finally leads to a divorce. At the political level, it manifests itself due to the changing foreign policy.

The opening scene of the novel finds Simrit surrounded by an artificial and snobbish life led by the elite of Delhi. One becomes aware of the corruption and hypocrisy pervading the social and political scene, which forms a backdrop of the novel. Nayantara successfully brings out the inner and outer contradictions and distortions of the Indian life. One strongly senses the apparent disorders and chaos at all levels. She believes in freedom at all levels and the doctrine of peaceful existence. The novel affirms faith in life and its immense potential through the character of Simrit. Speaking for her, the author states :

> From the high spot an immense valley of choices spread out before her gaze and she felt free at last to choose what her life would be. She was filled with sheer rightness of being alive and healthy at this particular time...[4]

Nayantara Sahgal's earlier novels are a realistic record of Indian struggle for freedom and its aftermath and the changing social and political scene. She is not only aware of the changes, but also their impact on the individual sensibility and collective life of the Indian psyche. Her vision is, however, not restricted as her final concern is with human values and man's destiny. Indian culture with its past traditions, the present issues and the future trends— nothing escapes her all—pervading vision. She does not believe in blindly clinging to the outworn traditions. She is liberal, humanistic and cosmopolitan in her outlook and gives space for human beings to grow. Her concept of freedom is not merely political. It includes the full expression of one's personality and discovering of one's true identity. Her characters show faith in an individual's capacity to communicate and reach others through debate and discussion. She believes that all progress, whether social, political or economic, is possible in an atmosphere of freedom and where people can communicate on all fronts. Having been brought up and nurtured under the impact of Gandhian ideology and Nehru's faith in the human spirit, she projects immense possibilities of life.

Jasbir Jain feels that "Her work has a strong realistic base and reflects not only her personal values but also the changing values of the society exposed for the first time to both freedom and power."[5] According to A.V. Krishna Rao, "Nayantara Sahgal is perhaps one of our best socio-political novelists to-day. She is authentic and vivid in rendering the contemporary Indian urban culture with all its inherent contradictions and imposed controversies."[6]

REFERENCES

1. Nayantara Sahgal, *A Time to be Happy* (Sterling Publishers Pvt. Ltd., New Delhi, 1975), p. 269.
2. ——*This Time of Morning* (Hind Pocket Books (P) Ltd., New Delhi, .), p. 221.
3. ——*Storm in Chandigarh* [Hind Pocket Books (P) Ltd., New Delhi, 1970], p. 1.
4. ——*The Day in Shadow* (Vikas Publishing House Pvt. Ltd., New Delhi, 1976), p. 236.
5. Jasbir Jain, *Nayantara Sahgal* [Arnold Heinemann Publishers (India) Pvt. Ltd., New Delhi, 1978], p. 9.
6. A.V. Krishna Rao, *Nayantara Sahgal* (M. Seshachalam and Co., Madras, 1976), p. 6.

11

Failure and Frustration : A Study of Anita Desai's 'In Custody'

A.N. DWIVEDI

Anita Desai, the most 'poetic novelist' of all in the contemporary arena, seems to have written her latest novel, *In Custody* (1984), in a mood of gloom and disenchantment over human frailty and predicament. *The Times Literary Supplement* has remarked that her protagonist's "extreme sensitivity never alienates the reader" and that she handles her plot with "narrative suspense"[1], but one wonders whether these remarks are applicable to this novel. Frankly speaking, we have neither the protagonist's 'extreme sensitivity' nor the 'narrative suspense' herein. The protagonist of the novel, Deven, is confronted with failure and frustration at every step, and is clearly sad, bitter and sardonic unto the last. Several obstructions come his way, and he does not know how to overcome them. He is the only character with whom the reader has some kind of sympathy, but he is befooled and cheated everywhere. The blurb page informs us that "*In Custody* is a sad, bitter, funny novel full of insight into human frailty and with some truly memorable scenes of comic catastrophe."[2] From this statement we may infer that it is none-too-happy a novel, that is 'funny' and about 'human frailty', and that only some of its scenes are 'truly memorable', and not all.

According to the noted British novelist E.M. Forster, a novel usually has at least three components—plot (story-

telling), people (characters) and pattern (design). Other
things like setting and conversation are only secondary.
Forster also makes a subtle distinction between 'plot' and
'story', and observes that "The king died and then the
queen died", is a story' whereas "The king died, and then
the queen died of grief" is a plot.[3] Viewed in the light of
Forster's essential components, *In Custody* fails to convince
us as a novel.

Consisting of eleven chapters and 204 pages and dedicated to Alicia Yerburgh, *In Custody* has a fragile thread to
hold it together. An impoverished, young College lecturer
in Hindi named Deven comes from Delhi and settles down
at Mirpore, a small town, along with his sullen and disappointed wife Sarla and small son Monu. He leads an
unhappy domestic life. The place he lives in looks like a
"cruel trap or prison"[4] for him. He discovers to his
dismay that his surroundings are not in consonance with
his high aspirations. His friend Murad arrives from Delhi
and tracks him out at his College. Both go out for lunch
in a bazaar restaurant and discuss their financial problems.
Deven complains to Murad about the non-payment for his
contributions—poems and reviews—to the latter's Urdu
magazine, *Awaaj*, but Murad silences him by saying that
his magazine has not been a success. He advises Deven
to interview the noted Urdu poet, Nur Shahjehanabadi, for
the forthcoming special issue of his magazine, and by
agreeing to his proposal Deven falls into his well-laid trap,
from which he can never escape. With a good deal of
hesitation, Deven goes to meet Nur at Delhi. The latter
rebukes him for being a lecturer in Hindi and yet interviewing a Urdu poet. Deven finds the atmosphere at Nur's
home quite suffocating, cruel and vulgar. Nur's wife scolds
the poet for drinking too much and the visitor for being
selfish. Deven runs away from there in a huff. But the
meddling Murad persuades him again to go and interview
Nur with courage and determination. Reaching Nur's, Deven
sees that a soiree-party has been arranged there to celebrate
the birth day of his second wife, Imtiaz-Bibi, who bores
the audience by her melodramatic and third-rate verses.

Nur and Deven leave the soiree half-way and secretly retire to a room, where Nur reveals to the interviewer that Imtiaz has cheated him of all his belongings, including the audience. Meanwhile, the two wives of Nur appear there and start quarelling most ferociously, and Deven has to flee from them. Once again Murad advises him to take the assistance of a tape-recorder in collecting the speeches and recitations of Nur and later edit them. Deven may even write a book like *My Days with Nur Shahjehanabadi* or a biography of Nur. The idea of tape-recorder clicks and Deven seeks the help of Mr Siddiqui, the Head of the Urdu Department at his College, in arranging funds for it. Murad persuades Deven to purchase a secondhand tape-recorder from the shop of Mr Jain, with whom Murad has a secret deal. A raw technician, Chiku, is provided to assist him in recording. But a revealing interview of the poet is a remote possibility owing to the high temperature and diarrhoea of Imtiaz-Begum. The first wife Safiya Begum, however, comes to the rescue of Deven and arranges his meeting with Nur at a hidden place. Chiku being a fool does not put the tape on and off, as required, during the entire conversation of Nur with Deven. He is more interested in his leave for home, in his sister's marriage, than in recording. The hard work of about three weeks goes wasted due to lack of technical expertise. Even the pruning of undesirable portions of the recorded tape does not succeed. The shop-owner, Mr Jain, allots another technician, Pintu, to him. Any real help in the matter comes from his disciples like Dhanu who are trained in radio technology and electronics; they cut undesirable portions and sounds from the cassettes. Even then the recording remains a patchwork which is "completely useless from a scholarly point of view."[5] In the mean time, letters from Nur keep pouring in for financial assistance— now for cataract operation, now for family maintenance, now for clearance of a bill of room-rent. Deven also receives a letter from Imtiaz-Begum, complaining of his utter ignorance of her poetic talent. When he approaches Murad for payment of some money for his contributions to

his magazine, the latter gives him a blunt reply, informing
him of the excessive bills on drinks and other materials
from hotels and restaurants he himself has received and
desiring the sole rights of the tape-recordings to sell them
to HMV or Polydor in order to clear his bills and debts.
Thus, Deven finds no truly sympathetic soul to console him
or to draw him out of the woods. Instead, he meets
failure and frustration from the beginning of the story to
the end. The reader of the novel is left with the impression that the entire story is spun out just to trap the protagonist, just to put him in a cage—"Still it was just a cage
in a row of cages. Cage, cage. Trap, trap."[6] The plot is
as indistinct and labyrinthine at the beginning as at the
end. The beginning depicts the two friends, Murad and
Deven, meeting each other in the College canteen beset
with stares and noises (where they can't sit or talk properly), and the end shows the latter panting for breath,
having an anxious morning walk, and pulling a branch of
thorns from under his foot.

As for characterization, we do not have fully developed
and three-dimensional characters in this novel, with the
possible exception of Deven. As a protagonist, he is seen
thrown from one problem to another, from one torture to
another, without getting any solution or relief. He is drawn
deeper and deeper into the project of interviewing India's
greatest Urdu poet, Nur, but is befooled, cheated and
bullied by all around him—by Nur's two wives, by the
shifty Murad, by shopkeepers, amateur technicians, threat-
ening students, and by the poet himself. Nur's verse
having sustained Deven since his childhood ultimately
lands him into troubles. The protagonist becomes an
embodiment of failure and frustration in pursuing his
ambitious project, and it is through him that the novelist's
'insight into human frailty' may be sensed. If Mrs Desai's
purpose was to present a really sad, bitter, and funny
novel, this purpose is fulfilled to a large extent by the
character of Deven, whose main fault seems to lie in his
childhood fancy, which he can neither control nor overcome at this stage. The inevitable result is sneer and deri-

sion from all, even from his employers, friends like Siddiqui
and officials like the Principal and the Head of the Department. His dismissal from the College service and the
recovery of debts and bills from him are also imminent.
Those whom he expects to assist him—like Murad and
Siddiqui—come forward with gibes and ironical remarks.

The selfishness of the Urdu poet, Nur, his wives Safiya
and Imtiaz, and Murad is quite evident in the course of this
novel. Nur is no more a celebrity ; he is now a 'dissolute
and rambling old man' residing in the bazaars of old Delhi
and seized with weak eyesight and senility. He is now
worried about his means of livelihood and tries to extort
money from Deven for interviewing and recording him.
His wives are garrulous and self-centred. Of the two,
Safiya keeps a low profile. Imtiaz claims to be a nature-
gifted poetess of talent and laments that Deven has not
understood her properly. If Nur demands money from
Deven for his cataract operation, the housewives send him
bills for room-rent and medical treatment of the son. And
Murad is a very cunning and crafty fellow. It is he who
prompts Deven to have the interview of Nur and to record
his speeches and recitations for the special number of his
magazine. His motive is clearly selfish ; he wants to pro-
mote the cause of his magazine and Urdu readers at the ex-
pense of Deven. He also exploits him in the purchase of the
old and outworn tape-recorder, being in secret league with
Jain Sahib, the shop-owner. And when Deven approaches
him for some payment for his contributions to his magazine, he starts shouting belligently at him, saying ''Don't
you try more of that on me. I've already spent every
paisa I could get from my mother on that blasted poet of
yours—''[7]. Even the attitude of the two technicians—
Chiku and Pintu—towards Deven is perfectly selfish and
money-oriented. While Chiku is quite inefficient and
ignorant about his work, being more interested in leave and
marriage of his sister, Pintu is slightly better and yet unable to set the records right. Deven's students assist him
in anticipation of good marks, but once they know where
they stand they hold out threats and abuses for him.

Surrounded by such a pack of hounds from all sides, it is
no wonder that Deven is totally crushed and depressed.
Of course, Deven as an intelligent man knows the cause of
his ruin and destruction, and he tells Siddiqui Sahib that
"it was not my fault ! I worked hard...but I was fooled
and cheated by everyone—the man who sold me the
secondhand equipment, the technician who said he could
do the recording but was completely inexperienced, by
Murad who said he would pay and did not, by Nur who
had never told me he wanted to be paid, and by his wife,
wives, all of them—."[8] But his knowledge does not help
him, and he is haunted down by adverse circumstances
like Hardy's Henchard in *The Mayor of Casterbridge*. We
only wish, someone should come his way and help him
out, but this is not to be !

The pattern of the novel is geared up towards the gradual unfolding of the calamities and perplexities of Deven. He
is its focal point and nerve-centre. The entire plot—what
Aristotle calls 'action' in a play—rotates round him; he is
to be seen at the begnining, middle and end of the novel.
Other characters in it—Nur, his wives, Murad, Jain Sahib,
etc.—play a subordinate role. We may say, they are just
the cogs in the wheel. The remaining characters really do
not matter much,—the technicians, the Principal, Mr Siddiqui, Mr Sharma, even the protagonist's wife Sarla and his
son Manu, the students, etc. Of course, Mrs Desai makes
a notable departure here and creates a male protagonist
instead of a female protagonist, as usual with her, but that
alone does not change her general attitude towards mankind. There is the same agony, the same sadness, the
same helplessness on the part of the protagonist here as
elsewhere.[9] Even the prose remains poetic and musical here
as in other novels, for example, "There was such a sound
of splashing and spilling then, of clinking and clattering, of
sloshing and giggling, one might have been quite misled
as to the seriousness of this annual affair."[10] Such examples may easily be multiplied from the text. Mostly the
novelist resorts to the method of description and narration
in this piece of fiction, but sometimes she also takes the

help of dialogues in furthering the story and portraying the character. Wherever she makes use of dialogues, they become sharp and revealing, occasionally even ironical and biting. At the very opening of the novel, we have the following incisive dialogue between Deven and Murad over the detaining of a devoted teacher from his class :

> 'But it's Monday-Not on Monday, Murad'.
> 'Oh, so friendship is only for Sunday, is it ?
> Is that friendship ?'
> Murad boomed.[11]

How ironical in his remarks Mr Siddiqui is when he hears the re-play of tape-recording in the staff-room ! He terms it as 'Charming' and smiles at Deven and rises from the sofa, indicating thereby that he has no more patience for it. He simply asks in a voice, "Deven, is that all ?"[12] This is certainly an instance of the novelist's understatement and terseness. As usual, Mrs Desai divides her novel into chapters, but one feels that it would have been better had she given titles or sub-titles to them. That would have rendered the pattern more accessible and intelligible; that would have made a reading of the novel easier and happier. By pointing out certain shortcomings in the novel, I do not intend denigrating Anita Desai as a novelist or her craftsmanship. Mrs Desai can undoubtedly build 'a mountain-like novel on a mole-hill like story'. I also do not wish to show that she totally fails in her artistic design and fictional mission in the writing of this novel. If *In Custody* she wanted to depict a protagonist in utter 'failure and frustration', she has rather succeeded in it to some extent. Deven is definitely an unmistakable person who is waging a hard struggle with his insurmountable problems both at home and outside. The frequent breakdown of his plans and programmes at times raises him even to tragic heights, and his ceaseless struggle with the odds renders him adventurous and heroic, but the reader is surprised to see him helplessly slipping into the hands of mischief-mongers and conspirators and letting the situation go beyond his control. The amount of surprise is all the more increased by the knowledge that he is a well-read and well-ranked person—a lecturer in a College which is certainly a post of prestige and responsibility—and yet he allows others (like Murad, Nur and their entourage) to exploit him to the maximum. And the irony of the whole thing is that he pays no heed to the sound and worthwhile advice of his friends and admirers. By way of contrast, the novelist shows other intelligent persons busy in house-construction, contract work, or College build-up, and Mr Siddiqui, the Head of the Urdu Department at the same College, is a living example of it, but this is not enough to open the eyes of Deven himself. He lives in a dream-wo ld, behaves like an innocent angel, and in the end faces a hostile world of harsh realities around him. The whole dream-world crumbles and disappears by slow degrees before his vision, and he is eventually left a pathetic and helpless creature in the midst of millions. What is being suggested here is the truth that Deven is far-removed from the world reality and commonsense and that he is not so practical as he ought to have been. Prof R.S. Sharma's observation that "Her [Mrs Desai's] protagonists are usually sensitive women who, haunted by a peculiar sense of doom, withdraw into a sequestered world of their own"[13] may also be applied to Deven with some reservations, for he is a sensitive man haunted by an overpowering sense of failure and frustration. The change of sex in protagonist does not bring a change in the artistic pattern of Anita Desai, who continues to write intensely, with "the sensitivity and imagination of a poet".[14] Her artistic drive goes with an amazing skill and intensity which demands a highly soaring imagination, and in the process she loosens her grip over her plot or story-line.[15] While her gifts as a prose stylist are now established on a sound footing' it is to be noted that her fictional canvas remains too small to be convincing.[16] Like Jane Austen, she carves out designs and patterns on 'two inches of ivory', and seems to be lost in the exploration of the complex mental moods and psychic states of her dominant charact ers. By the time the harsh realities of life impinge upon her consciousness and shatter her dream-world abounding in music and poetry, it is too late to revert to the conditions of a happy living for them.

Even Anita Desai is not unaware of the thinness of her plot or story-line. In her interview given to Dr Atma Ram, she makes the following illuminating statement :

> I start writing without having very much of a 'plot' in my mind or on paper—only a very hazy idea of what the pattern of the book is to be. But it seems to work itself out as I go along, quite naturally and inevitably. I prefer the word 'pattern' to 'plot' as it sounds—more natural— and even better, if I dare use it, is Hopkins' word 'inscape' —while 'plot' sounds arbitrary, heavy-handed and artificial, all that I wish to avoid. One should have a pattern and then fit the characters, the setting, and scenes into it—each piece in keeping with the others and so forming a balanced whole.[17]

The statement inevitably leads us to believe that Mrs Desai gives her attention more to those little things that combine to produce an experience than to incident or experience itself, that she lays her emphasis more on 'pattern and rhythm' than on 'plot', and that she is more concerned with the overall effects of a work of art, with the need of relating the parts to the whole, than with the artificial and arbitrary aspects of art. And in her practice, she is closer in spirit to a complex poet like G.M. Hopkins than to the straightforward story-teller Thomas Hardy (who invariably wrote with a clear-cut idea of his 'plot', which scholars have termed as his 'architectonic'). Instead of stressing any other essential component of E.M. Forster, Mrs Desai has chosen 'pattern and rhythm', which "implies a balance, a synthesis and proportion."[18] So, *In Custody* also falls in line with her other novels in its slightness of plot and morbidity of recurrently agonising feeling and experiences.

To sum up, it may be said that *In Custody* is a novel abounding in failure and frustration, bitterness and restlessness, and that the protagonist in it constantly leads a life of mental and physical tortures and financial hardships. The noted Indo-English poet, K.N. Daruwalla, has also found fault with this sad and sarcastic novel. While reviewing it for *The Hindustan Times*, he remarks that the novel is "built around a non-issue",[19] and that its theme does not cope with its grand style. Commenting on the ending of the novel, he further remarks that "whether one takes it that Deven commits suicide or refrains from commiting it, frankly left me surprised and untouched."[20] Though serious problems may arise from trivial incidents—such as in Pope's *The Rape of the Lock* (1712 and 1714 editions), it is least convincing that a Hindi lecturer, an intelligent and grown-up man indeed, falls into the inescapable trap of some Urdu lovers like Murad and Nur, paying no heed to the warnings of his friends and well-wishers and incurring the wrath employers resulting in his dismissal from service and untold financial miseries. Deven's fanaticism exceeds all bounds of decency and decorum, and he must continue to live in his self-created Inferno.

REFERENCES

1. Cited from the back cover of *Cry the Peacock* (1963; New Delhi : Orient Paperbacks, 1980).
2. Quoted from the Jacket cover of *In Custody* (London : William Hienemann, 1984).
3. E.M. Forster, *Aspects of the Novel* (Harmondsworth, Middlesex : Penguin Books Ltd., 1936), p. 45.
4. Anita Desai, *In Custody*, p. 19.
5. *Ibid.*, p. 180.
6. *Ibid.*, p. 131.
7. *Ibid.*, p. 188.
8. *Ibid.*, p. 199.
9. As, for instance, Maya in *Cry, the Peacock* (1963), or Sita in *Where Shall We Go This Summer ?* (1975), or Nanda Kaul in *Fire on the Mountain* (1977).
10. *In Custody*, p. 95.
11. *Ibid.*, p. 9.
12. *Ibid.*, 181.
13. R.S. Sharma, *Anita Desai* (New Delhi : Arnold-Heinemann, 1981), p. 166,
14. *Ibid.*
15. R.S. Sharma rightly remarks:
    Nothing escapes her eyes, not even the leg of a spider! This intensity and density of texture compensates for the absence of a strong plot or story line in her fiction. One reads her novels like long poems drawn mostly from those corners of life where no poverty seems to exist (p. 166).

16. *Ibid.,* p. 167.
17. Atma Ram, "An Interview with Anita Desai", *WLWE,* XVI, No. 1 (April 1977), p. 101.
18. *Ibid.,* p. 100.
19. Keki N. Daruwalla, "Built on a Non-Issue", *The Hindustan Times* (Sunday Magazine, 13th January 1985).
20. *Ibid.*

12

Existentialist Overtones in Anita Desai's Fire on the Mountain

S.M. KHANNA

First published in 1977, *Fire on the Mountain* is the fifth novel of Anita Desai. She was awarded the Sahitya Academy Award in 1978, soon after its publication. In this novel, it is held, Mrs Desai "again handles, as she has done in all her earlier novels, an existentialist theme with consummate delicacy and dexterity." Mrs Desai "explores the inner emotional world, which is the hall mark of existentialist literature, of a great-grandmother, Nanda Kaul, with a rare poignancy".[2] Jasbir Jain has laid emphasis on Mrs Desai's preoccupation with the emotional world by calling her novels 'Stairs to the Attie'. The purpose of this paper is to examine the validity of these appraisals with special references to *Fire on the Mountain*

Existentialism can be best defined as an attitude to-wards life based upon a kind of philosophical analysis of the modern human predicament. Yet the modernity of existentialism as a school of philosophy is more apparent than real. Problems of human existence have always interested philosophers and social workers. Kierkegaard, the father of modern existentialism, was not the first thinker to rebel against doctrinaire philo-sophy. He is one of the best known because he asked the right type of questions about human existence at the right time with a purely modernist stance. The burgeoning economic, biological and spiritual determinism of the 19th century created an unprecedented crisis in the history of human existence. The two world wars in the 20th century and their impact on the upper-middle class intellectuals completely undermined the traditional values and deprived existence of all its meaning.

Sartre, admittedly one of the most extreme existentialists, has tried to establish, through existentialism, a philosophy of individual responsibility. He comes to hold that "Even though the world may seem absurd, man must create purpose for himself, using his ability to the uttermost."[3] Sartre represents a philosophical reaction to the idealistic determinism of Hegel, who held that man is not a free agent, nor has he ever been ; he is merely a canny creature capable of deluding himself into poetic notions of liberty, to forget the tyrannical consciousness of helplessness and to obliterate the frightening awareness of his limitations and dependence on others, and especially to obviate the all-consuming fear of death. Hegel's postulate of the dialectical relationship between the individual consciousness and society or his environment suffered a sea-change in the mind of Karl Marx and the existentialists reacted in an extreme manner by overemphasizing the importance of the individual. It is in the light of this school of existentialism that we must examine *Fire on the Mountain*.

It is said that "The existential attitude begins with a disoriented individual facing a confused world that he cannot accept."[4] This is an attitude of self-consciousness in which man feels himself separated from the world and from other people. It is an attitude that alienates the people of the world as well as an individual of that world.

John Macquarrie, in his book entitled *Existentialism*, lays emphasis on freedom, decision, responsibility, finitude, guilt, alienation, despair, death, anxiety, boredom, nausea, the emotional life of human beings, time as the fourth dimension, interpersonal relations, the problem of truth, nihilism, lostness, thrownness, etc. as the main themes, recurring in most of the existentialist thinkers.

Jean-Paul Sartre was among the first existentialist writers to maintain that emotions are conscious acts, purposive and meaningful ways of constituting our world. He insists that our emotions are meaningful. Sartre, agreeing half-way with Hegal, is of the view that although man is incapable of changing the world, he can nevertheless change the direction of consciousness, intentions and behaviour. Thus the emotions can 'transform the world'. He quotes an example from Aesop's tales. A man desirous to pick a bunch of grapes, when unable to get at them, calls them 'sour'. This change is brought about because of the change in his attitude. ''So it is with all emotions. In order to cope with frustration, they change our view of a world we cannot change.''[5]

If we judge *Fire on the Mountain* from this definition of existentialism and the recurring theme thereof, as pointed out by John Macquarrie, we find that Anita Desai is, undoubtedly, an existentialist Indian novelist in English but with a flaw. Her purpose is to adroitly explore the emotional life of her characters, especially female characters, in her novels, but unfortunately she chooses only those characters who are emotionally furnished and who have turned renegades, having failed to come to terms with reality. They choose to live in the cell of the self, building up a world of fantasy. Their preoccupation with the self becomes an obsession with them. All human relations which are the best means of nourishing our emotions, have turned meaningless for these emotionally famished characters of *Fire on the Mountains*—Nanda Kaul, Raka and Ila Das. Each one of them is a victim of emotional alienation and craves for privacy, isolation and fantasy to escape from unpleasant reality of life.

The novel is pervaded by an overpowering sense of loneliness and isolation in the deserted life of the protagonist, Nanda Kaul. The novel portrays a reverberating and pathetic picture of old age. Nanda Kaul, an old lady, lives a life of a recluse in her village at Carignano in the Simla hills. Ramlal is the only other person who keeps and cooks for Nanda Kaul in the house. Carignano is exactly to Napda Kaul's expectations and liking. Its 'barrenness' and 'its starkness' please her most. She has preferred to live at Carignano because she does not wish her privacy to be disturbed at any cost :

> Everything she wanted was here, at Carignano, in Kasuli. Here, on the ridge of the mountain in this quiet house. It was the place, and the time of life, that she had wanted and prepared for all her life — as she realised on her first day at Carignano, with a great, cool flowering of relief — and at last she had it. She wanted no one and nothing else. Whatever else came, or happened here, would be an unwelcome intrusion and distraction.[6]

Nanda Kaul's reading of *A Woman Lives Alone* from the Pillow Book of Sri Shonagon is in the fitness of the natural setting of the novel. Her desire for privacy is so domineering that the very sight of the postman, slowly approaching the house, arouses ripples of irritation in her quiet mind :

> The sight of him, inexorably closing in with his swollen bag; rolled a fat ball of irritation into the cool cave of her day, blocking it stupidly : bags and letters, messages and demands, requests, promises and queries, she had wanted to be done with them all, at Carignano. She asked to be left to the pines and cicadas alone (p. 3).

This state of desirelessness, wanting no one and nothing else, is absolutely deceptive as well as resultant of the human predicament in practical life. Quite reluctantly, Nanda Kaul takes the letter from the postman. The letter is from her daughter Asha. It breaks the news of the arrival of a new-comer named Raka, Nanda Kaul's great-granddaughter, at Carignano. This is the most unwelcome news to Nanda Kaul. Her angst to get rid of the new responsibility is explicit from her own words :

> Have I not done enough and had enough ? I want no more. I want nothing. Can I not be left with nothing ? (p. 17).

These short sentences reveal the agitated state of Nanda Kaul's mind. When in anger or in excitement, one never bursts in lengthy sentences.

Nanda Kaul is living in an atmosphere of self-imposed exile at Carignano. She is completely fed up with a life full of responsibilities in the same nausiating duties of family cares and chores which, with the arrival of Raka, came to disturb her 'inner vacuous emotional world' and her illusory calmness at Carignano :

> Now to bow again, to let the noose slip once more round her neck that she had thought was freed fully, finally. Now to have those walls and bawls shatter and rip her still house to pieces . . . Now to converse again when it was silence she wished, to question and follow up and make sure of another's life and comfort and order, to involve oneself, to involve another (p. 19).

Raka's arrival at Carignano is a threat to Nanda Kaul's consciously guarded 'privacy'. She hates the nasty thought of 'opening of that old, troublesome ledger again ? She finds it painfully difficult to re-enter the business of living. Her deep agony is remarkably delineated :

> Hanging her head miserably, it seemed too much to her that she should now have to meet Raka, discover her as an individual and, worse, as a relation, a dependent. She would have to urge her to eat eggs and spinach, caution her against lifting stones in the garden under which scorpions might lie asleep, see her to bed at night and lie in the next room, wondering if the child slept, straining to catch a sound. . .
>
> She would never be able to sleep, Nanda Kaul moaned to herself, how could she sleep with someone else in the house, it would upset her so (p. 35).

As the wife of the Vice-Chancellor, Nanda Kaul managed the household chores with great skill. The irony is that she, with all her children, grand children and great grand children, feels herself absolutely alienated even in her own house, "Mentally she stalked through the rooms of that house, never hers" Nanda Kaul's alienation with her husband is the most unpleasant fact of her life but she deliberately suppresses it in the sub-conscious mind. Instead of fighting for the restoration of her rights, she brings about a change in her attitude and accepts the reality as it is in a sadistic manner. We are told :

> Nor had her husband loved and cherished her and kept her like a queen-he had only done enough to keep her quiet while, he carried on a lifelong affair with Miss David, the mathematics mistress, whom he had not married because she was a Christian but whom he had loved, all his life loved. And her [Nanda Kaul's] child-ren—The children were all alien to her nature. She neither understood nor loved them. She did not live here alone by choice. She lived here alone because that was what she was forced to do, reduced to doing (p. 145).

Nanda Kaul tries to obliterate the unhappy memory of a married life not only by burying it in the subconscious but also by deliberately trying to create a happy world of fantasy. This becomes clear to us when she tells Raka about the imaginary happy household kept by her father : "Yes, Yes," the old lady would say :

> "What splendid times. There was stream. You know, at the back of the house, lined with poplars and willows, where our ducks and geese swam...

> All round the house was an orchard. Mostly apple trees, but my father was fond of experimenting..., he grafted a plum tree out a peach and the result was a most curious and delightful fruit—the skin downy, like a peach, only one bit into it and found it plum (p. 93).

Unfortunately, Nanda Kaul finds a horrifying symbolism in this yarn spun by her. Really, it was not a plum tree that her father had grafted onto a peach ; it was really his emotionally famished daughter Nanda Kaul, whom he had grafted onto a highly emotional and promising youngman who later became a Vice-Chancellor. The marriage appear-ed quite attractive like the downy skin of the peach. But when Nanda Kaul tried to have a bite at it, her teeth simply caught the stone of the plum and left a bitter taste of life that still lingered. Far from being a happy wife, she felt like an animal put into a cage and very cruelly trained to dance and turn antics at the command of the ring-master, her domineering husband, whom she could not defy. Her fabricated narrative communicated to Raka is only an attempt to bury the past under the fantasy created in the present. It was her failure to attain fulfilment in marriage and other human relations that had brought her to Carignano.

Nanda Kaul's relationship with Ila Das has an astonishing ambivalence. She is her friend, the only one still quite close to her and yet she is also a living reminder of her unhappy past. She had great sympathy for her at one time, but now her presence torments her like a guilty conscience. Ila Das symbolises Nanda Kaul's past that has inevitably telescoped into the present. Nanda Kaul unconsciously desires to destroy this haunting past, but she does not know that the past, the present and the future are organically linked together. Her desire to delink her past from her present ultimately results in her death, immediately after hearing the death of Ila Das.

Raka, whose arrival at Carignano was apprehended as unwelcome, proves to be quite unlike other children Nanda Kaul had known. Raka's imaginary world reflects her alienation from the disjointed world of her parents. This 'freak' child is in the habit of 'never making a demand.' She too, like her great-grandmother, loves a life of loneliness :

> Raka was not like any other child she had known, not like any of her own children or grandchildren. Amongst them, she appeared a freak by virtue of never making a demand. She appeared to have no needs ... like her own grandmother, Raka wanted only one thing—to be left alone and pursue her own secret life amongst the rocks and pines of Kasauli (pp. 47-48).

Nanda Kaul finds that Raka is her own true copy in respect of temperament. She asks Raka : "You really are a great grandchild of mine, aren't you ? You are more like me than any of my children or grandchildren. You are exactly like me, Raka" (p. 64). This sameness of temperament is evident at each step. But Nanda Kaul was a recluse out of vengeance for a long life of duty and obligation and her great-grand-daughter was a recluse by nature, by instinct (p. 48).

In her delineation of Raka, Anita Desai strikes a rather false and confusing note. As the narrative gradually un- folds itself, we find that Raka is a recluse neither by nature nor by instinct. It is the domestic violence that has alienat- ed her from her parents and other children. For her, every human relationship is dreadful. The festive orgy at the Club opens the floodgates of her unconscious and repres- sed, unhappy memories of early childhood, which burst out in the form of a nightmare :

> A whimper burst from Raka then, like a whimper from a pod or a bud when it is pricked or pressed and bursts, Shooting out of the corner like a seed from the burst pod, she...fled like an animal chased, sobbing 'Hate them-hate them... somewhere behind them, behind it all, was her father, home from a party, stumbling and crashing through the curtains of night, his mouth open- ing set out a flood of rotten stench, beating at her mother with hammers and fists of abuse-harsh, filthy abuse that made Raka cover under her bedclothes and wet the mattress in fright, feeling the stream of urine warm and weakening between her legs like a stream of blood and her mother lay down on the floor and shut her eyes and wept (pp. 71-72).

It would be, however, rather naive to suppose that the child Raka sought an existentialist solution of her frightened misery in her love of solitude. She avoided company just on account of her deep-rooted fear.

The unmarried and lonely Ila Das has been presented as a foil to Nanda Kaul, though both of them share the same predicament. Ila Das was born in a prosperous family and had a very happy childhood, enriched by the love of all. But the family disintegrated after her father's death. The husband of her friend Nanda Kaul was the Vice-Chance- llor and he very kindly appointed her as a lecturer in a Home Science College. After the Vice-Chancellor's death, however, she is denied justice and some junior lecturer is made the Principal in her place. This intensively hurts her and she resigns thinking that 'it was the only honourable thing to do,' She has, thereafter, "to go from pillar to post, trying to earn fifty rupees here and fifty rupees there, with not a room to call my own most of the time and it's grown worse and worse'' (p. 125).

Ila Das, who is a Welfare Officer in the Himalayan Foothills, is devoted and sincere to her profession. She forbids the villagers, among whom she serves, to practise superstitions and social evils like child-marriage. She, however, finds herself alienated from the people and she has to struggle hard with the villagers. She relates her efforts to Nanda Kaul :

> Now I've just heard about a family living in my own village—they're planning to marry their little girl, who is only just seven, to an old man in the next village because he owns a quarter of an acre of land and two goats. He is a widower and has six children but...But he's a sullen lout, I could see I wasn't making any headway with him (pp. 129-30).

This reveals that she is very much alert to the sense of freedom, freedom from the ills that are spreading contagion in her rootless society. For this dare-devil effort, she has to pay a very heavy price. She is in a hurry to retire to her hut before it gets dark, but Preet Singh, waiting eagerly for the opportunity, pounces upon her and criminally assaults and murders her. This criminal assault committed on her and the subsequent murder are symbolic of the simultaneous fulfilment of her unconscious craving for married life and the subsequent death-wish, engendered by the frustration of this emotional craving.

The telephonic message of the rape and murder of Ila Das gives a rude shock to Nanda Kaul, who, unable to bear it, collapses forthwith. Her long-cherished death-wish is, thus, finally fulfilled. It is obvious from the above analysis that Nanda Kaul and her great-grand daughter Raka are living in a world of fantasy, far from the maddening crowd. But this escape from the mundane realities of life is no solution to the prevailing existentialist problems. Nanda Kaul builds a magnificent edifice of fantasy. But this pleasant edifice tumbles down like a house of cards when she gets the tragic news of the rape and murder of Ila Das.

Both the language and imagery of the novel have a subjective existentialist tone. Nanda Kaul is always reluctant to receive letters because they bring some news and the news is only about trouble, danger and problems. It gives her the notion that she is living in a terrible and frightening world—a world full of catastrophies, a world where everything threatens her safety. She cannot stand this world. It appears absurd and incoherent to her, but she fails to adopt the existentialist heroic posture, necessary to face it. She simply tries to constantly push it away from herself and to forget all about it instead of facing it squarely. The world round Carignano is stark and barren. The imagery used to describe this world and its inhabitants is obsessive. It is the imagery of snakes, scorpions, lizards, crickets, escapist cicadas and gibbering langoors. Nanda Kaul's escapist immersion into herself has turned Kasauli into a waterland, where almost everything is barren and stark.

Existentialism is basically a philosophy of revolt against the unimpeded encroachment of society on the self of the individual, but there is no indication of any such revolt in *Fire on the Mountain.* Both Nanda Kaul and Ila Das succumb to the problems of their existence like helpless creatures. They do not succeed in lending any authenticity to their existence. Koestenboum says : "Existentialism holds man fully responsible for his actions and inactions : it does not displace blame onto upbringing, heredity and environment". This we do not find in *Fire on the Mountain.* Of the two main orientations among existentialists comprising, viz. (a) concern with changing directly the outer conditions of man's lives—a kind of external rebellion which has been preached by Sartre ; and (b) a concern with altering society indirectly through changes man can effect in himself, which has been exemplified by Camus, Anita Desai does not accept either of these. She adopts the decadent type of existentialism that borders on nihilism.

REFERENCES

1. Madhusudan Prasad, *Anita Desai : The Novelist* (New Horizon, Allahabad, 1981), p. 78.
2. *Ibid.*, p. 78.
3. John C. Merrill, *Existentialism Journalism* (New York, 1977), p. 17.
4. Robert C. Solemon, *Hegel to Existentialism* (O.U.P, 1987), p. 238.
5. *Ibid.*, p. 267.
6. Anita Desai, *Fire on the Mountain* (Allied Publishers Pvt. Ltd., New Delhi, 1985), p. 3.

All subsequent textual references have been given parenthetically.

13

Arun Joshi and the Gita

O. P. MATHUR

The *Gita* is not merely a scripture but a universal document which embodies men's perpetual doubts, withdrawals, quests and involvements as much as an affirmation of faith. The prime emphasis of the *Gita* is on man and how he should act. The question it raises and the answer it provides are both of a fundamental nature and universal relevance. To quote S. Radhakrishnan :

> The *Bhagavadgita* recognizes the nature of man, the needs of man, and tries to fulfil all of them....The metaphysical quest, the religious inquiry, starts with this experience of the evanescence, the transitoriness of life, the tyranny of time to which we are all subject. We ask : Is time all ? Is death all ? Is annihilation all ? Or is there a timeless element ? Is there a deathless element, an element which devours death...?[1]

Such questions underlie much of serious fiction and make the study of *Bhagawadgita* of perennial importance for all those who are concerned with the basic problems of human life and conduct.

Among the contemporary Indian English novelists, Arun Joshi has highlighted most effectively some of the eternal metaphysical and ethical questions. Any Indian novelist who does so can hardly avoid the deep and everlasting impact of the *Gita* on Indian life and thought. In Arun Joshi's case, this impact is not casual or co-incidental: it seems to form the philosophical and ethical fabric of some of his major work. He has unambiguously referred to the *Gita* and its message more than once, and the anguish, the dilemma, the quest and the arrival, in brief, in his own words, "that mysterious underworld which is the human soul,"[2] find a voice in his tortured fiction.

Arun Joshi's first novel, *The Foreigner*, presents a protagonist who undergoes a sort of spiritual transformation. The relevance of some of the concepts of the *Gita*—action-inaction, attachment-detachment, involvement-noninvolvement—has been constantly shown in relation to the protagonist. At one place he goes to the extent of saying clearly: "Not many preach the *Gita* even as it is."[3] Sindi Oberoi himself is an embodiment of the evolution of a blundering approach to the concepts of the *Gita* into their truer understanding and practice. Sindi's early career is a travesty of the *Gita's* concept of non-attachment. In his actions he is portrayed as detached from the world, but his detachment leads to inaction illustrating the following verse of the *Gita* :

अनाश्रित: कर्मफलं कार्यं कर्म करोति य: ।
स संन्यासी च योगी च न निरग्निनं चाक्रिय: ।

(He who does the work which he ought to do without seeking its fruit he is the Samnyasin, he is the yogin, not he who does not light the sacred fire, and performs no rites).[4]

Having lost both his parents, who were Indians, at the age of four, Sindi gets his school education in Kenya, higher education in Engineering in England, and lands on a job in the United States. He is completely rootless and does not belong anywhere. This gives him a sense of detachment, which he seems to relish. The distorted faces in a cheap mirror behind a bar make him feel a lonely alien even in a crowded room as if he were sitting in his own tomb (p. 24). He declares that he has lost all faith even in himself as a free agency (p. 82). He realises that he

had learnt to be detached from the world but not from himself (p. 207). He makes love to June Blyth, but is haunted
by the meaninglessness of everything including his love.
He, therefore, does not reciprocate June's desire for marriage and she leaves him for another Indian friend of his,
Babu Rao Khemka, and later tells Sindi on phone that she
is going to marry Babu. A prisoner of his own "inaction,"
Sindi weeps into the telephone (pp. 138-39). Later, when
the frustrated June wants to return to Sindi, he tries to
comfort her and help her find herself by making love to
her, though again without any serious intent. This makes
her confess her love for Sindi to Babu, who, unable to bear
the shock, commits suicide, leaving June with child. Soon
after, she also dies in an attempted abortion. Thus, the confused approach of Sindi to the concept of detachment has
cost him two lives, both dear to him. The "detachment"
of the *Gita* does not mean inaction as Sindi takes it to
mean, Lord Krishna had warned Arjuna against inaction, and
the deaths of two persons closest to Sindi are a warning to
him which he fully understands :

> Detachment at that time had meant inaction. Now I had
> begun to see the fallacy in it. Detachment consisted
> of right action and not escape from it. The Gods had
> set a heavy price to teach me just that. (p. 204)

But it was not even detachment out of which Sindi had
made love to June. It was from, as he says, "merely a
desire to prove that I still held the key to June's happiness".

> I had presumed that I could extricate her from the web
> of her own actions : that I could make her happy by
> simply standing still and letting her use me whichever
> way she wished. Nothing could have been farther from
> the idea of detachment. That was a fatal presumption
> (p. 208).

Sindi seems to illustrate the *Rajasik* action defined in the
Gita (XIV.7).

The suicide of Babu and the death of June, both arising
from Sindi's confusion of attachment and detachment, mark
a turning point in his career and he decides to leave

America—but for which country, Nigeria or India ? The spin
of the coin in favour of India makes him happy at the prospect of his returning to the land of his ancestors. A thrill of
joy spreads through his body and he celebrates the occasion.   His initial feeling after arrival in India and after
seeing his employer Khemka (Babu's father) get into serious
trouble with Income Tax people, is that it has only been a
change of theatre from America and the show has remain-
ed unchanged (p. 220). He still wants to remain uninvolv-
ed.   He had confided to Sheila earlier :

> I withdraw from action for another reason.
> I first want to know the purpose of action.
> ... There is no purpose in life.   There is
> perhaps a little purpose in right action,
> in action without desire (p. 146).

His much-vaunted detachment ultimately crumbles down.
Two of the strongest passions known to man are aroused
in him—anger at Khemka's dishonest practices and love
for the suffering poor like Muthu who had been cheated by
Khemka.

> It was a sad sight. The workers' clothes were falling
> off in rags and sweat poured off their backs as if they
> had just had a shower. What was the point in all those
> big men like Mr Khemka talking about God and pain so
> long as half-naked men had to wrestle with a beastly
> mass of concrete under a scorching sun ?   And all for
> three rupees a day. These are my people, I thought. And
> yet I moved among them as if I were a stranger.[5]
> (p. 207).

Now at long last he reaches the right conclusion that for
him "detachment consisted in getting involved with the
world" (p. 239). He decides to accept the employees'
unanimous demand that he should take over the manage-
ment of the imprisoned Khemka's firm :

> As I entered the room I had a strange sensation, some-
> thing I had never before felt in life. I felt as if I had
> been dropped on a sinking ship and charged with the
> impossible task of taking it ashore. The men looked up
> at me unblinking, their expressionless faces reflecting

neither love nor scepticism, but only the accumulated despair of their weary lives. Until that moment I had not realized how considerably my visit to Muthu's home had affected me. If that was the sum total of Muthu's life God alone knew what massive suffering lay behind those vacant eyes. It almost overwhelmed me (pp. 239- 40).

Now Sindi, like Arjuna, surrenders to the right kind of in- volvement and the right kind of action with which his selfish desires have nothing to do. Realising the true nature of his situation, he gives a twist to his name "Surin- der" and calls himself "Surrender" (p. 242). This message of self-surrender is embodied in Chapter VIII verse 7 of the *Gita* on which Radhakrishnan comments, "All actions of our lives are to be surrendered to God who encloses, penetrates and gives meaning to our lives"[5] Reminiscing over his past and attempting to prognosticate the future, Sindi has realised :

> Before I went to sleep that night I took a general stock of myself. In many ways the past had been a waste, but it had not been without its lessons. I had started adult life as a confused adolescent, awesomely engros- sed with myself, searching for wisdom and the peace that comes with it. The journey had been long and tedi- ous and still was not over.
>
> And the future ? In an ultimate sense, I knew, it would be as meaningless as the past. But, in a narrower sense, there would perhaps be useful tasks to be done; perhaps, if I were lucky, even a chance to redeem the past (p. 234).

What Sindi had once said to June has now become the guiding principle of his life : "you can love without attach- ment, without desire. You can love without attachment to the objects of your love" (p. 180). Arun Joshi seems to condemn both existential detachment and involvement with the self which Sindi embodies in the earlier part of his life. The *Foreigner* underlines the importance of non- involvement with the self but a sympathetic involvement with the world as a step towards the achievement of

'Karmayoga' or non-attached action. Sindi's career seems to illustrate the truth of the following verses of the *Gita*.

न कर्मणामनारम्भान्नैष्कर्म्यं पुरुषोऽश्नुते ।
न च संन्यसनादेव सिद्धिं समधिगच्छति ।

(Not by abstention from work does a man attain freedom from action; nor by mere renunciation does he
attain to his perfection).

न हि कश्चित्क्षणमपि जातु तिष्ठत्यकर्मकृत् ।
कार्यते ह्यवशः कर्म सर्वः प्रकृतिजैर्गुणैः ॥

(For no one can remain even for a moment without
doing work; everyone is made to act helplessly by the
impulses born of nature.)

कर्मेन्द्रियाणि संयम्य य आस्ते मनसा स्मरन् ।
इन्द्रियार्थान्विमूढात्मा मिथ्याचारः स उच्यते ॥

(He who restrains his organs of action but continues in
his mind to brood over the objects of sense, whose
nature is deluded is said to be a hypocrite (a man of
false conduct).

यस्त्विन्द्रियाणि मनसा नियम्यारभतेऽर्जुन ।
कर्मेन्द्रियैः कर्मयोगमसक्तः स विशिष्यते ॥

(But he who controls the senses by the mind, O Arjuna,
and without attachment engages the organs of action in
the path of work, he is superior).

नियतं कुरु कर्म त्वं कर्म ज्यायो ह्यकर्मणः ।
शरीरयात्रापि च ते न प्रसिद्ध्येदकर्मणः ॥

(Do thou thy allotted work, for action is better than
inaction; even the maintenance of thy physical life cannot be effected without action).

यज्ञार्थात्कर्मणोऽन्यत्र लोकोऽयं कर्मबन्धनः ।
तदर्थं कर्म कौन्तेय मुक्तसङ्गः समाचर ।

(Save work done as and for a sacrifice this world is in
bondage to work. Therefore, O son of Kunti (Arjuna)
do thy work as a sacrifice becoming free from all attachment). (The *Gita*, III 4-9).

The concluding part of the novel seems to illustrate how
complete non-attachment can be easily attained by the

common man through the intermediary stage of involvement with the world and not with self, the gradual reaching out into light of a confused and benighted soul.
Through its protagonist. *The Foreigner* seems to demonstrate :

कर्मणो ह्यपि बोद्धव्यां बोद्धव्यं च विकर्मण: ।
अकर्मणश्च बोद्धःयं गहना कर्मणो गति: ।।

(One has to understand what action is, and likewise
one has to understand what is wrong action and one
has to understand about inaction. Ha·d to understand
is the way of work), (The *Gita*, IV, 17).

The Foreigner, thus, is a work of strong affirmation and
what Sindi learns from life and suffering is not much different from what Krishna had preached about the right type
of action.

The other novels of Arun Joshi embody different aspects
of the message of the *Gita*. The story of the strange case
of Billy Biswas is strange only to the uninitiated, the ones
who have lost contact with Nature in her primordial state,
the mother, the womb of all creatures. The protagonist
of Billy (Bimal) Biswas, who has studied, significantly,
Anthropology in place of Engineering to study which he
was sent to U.S.A., has not only developed a distaste for
the superficial glamour of the so-called civilized life, but
also feels a strong gravitation towards the tribal. He escapes from the prison of civilization into the freedom of
life in a primitive society only to be relentlessly pursued by
the well-meaning representatives of civilization to an un-
intentional death.

The 'strange' case may be taken as an allegory of the
realization of one's true self, "the final resolution" of one's
life, the meaning of which "lies not in the glossy surfaces
of our pretensions but in those dark mossy labyrinths of
the soul that languish forever, hidden from the dazzling
light of the sun " (p. 8). This contrast between the superficial and the real informs the whole work. The necessity
of leading an authentic life is often theoretically admitted.
But only rare sensitive souls like Billy are attuned to its

call. This irrepressible call of "a great force, *urkraft* a...a primitive force" (p. 23) makes him lose his identity: "Layer upon layer was peeled off me until nothing but my primitive self was left trembling in the moonlight." (p. 121). He is not sure whether he belongs to "the wilderness" or to "the marts of the Big City" (p. 96). He feels that his soul had all along been clamouring for "that other thing," which is "something like" God (p. 189). After finally becoming one with "wilderness," Billy is supposed to have attained magical powers which also point towards the necessity of some sort of faith in this rationalistic and mechanistic society which has made men like robots. Incidentally, the name of the hero, Bimal Biswas, also means "pure faith". An "occasional suspension of disbelief, combined with the opening up of one's heart to the breezes, the mountains and the stars can soothe the frayed nerves of the modern man. While glorifying the 'noble savage,' the novel enshrines the merger of the Purusa and Prakriti of the Sankhya Philosophy[6] and celebrates the nature-worship of the Vedas. Joshi has delineated the charming simplicity of an authentic life in a primitive society the virtues of which may act as a corrective to our money-based culture. The affirmations of this novel are of fundamental importance to us, though they are shrouded in symbols that may appear 'fantastic' to the 'civilized.'

The Apprentice, the shortest of Arun Joshi's novels, is a paradigm of the insufficiency of and the frustrations caused by a purely materialistic approach to life. The protagonist Ratan Rathor is caught in the meshes of his own confusions, leading to greed and corruption resulting in the death of his friend, the Brigadier, for which he himself is indirectly responsible, for it was he who was instrumental in the supply of defective ammunition resulting in the Brigadier's desertion and his consequent ignoring and suicide. This burdens him with the sorrow of a wasted life. Like Arjuna, a disciple of Lord Krishna, Ratan Rathor also ultimately becomes a sort of apprentice saying, "there are losses that one cannot readily accept. There are things, shorn of which, it is very difficult to die. Therefore, I say

let us give battle, howsoever late the hour."[7] Though a prosperous businessman, he starts his day by standing outside
a temple and cleaning the shoes of the devotees and saying to himself, "Be good.   Be decent.   Be of use," "Then,
"as he says, "I beg forgiveness. Of a large host : my father,
my mother, the Brigadier, the unknown dead of the war, of
those whom I harmed, with deliberation and with cunning,
of all those who have been the victims of my cleverness,
those whom I could have helped and did not." (pp. 148-
49). In his middle age he has become a spiritual apprentice and wants that younger persons should also be "willing to learn and ready to sacrifice." (p. 150). Ratan Rathor's
penance is not physical but spiritual. He is willing to pay
the price by suffering humiliation. The sacrifice that he
himself makes is something on the lines of the sacrifice
mentioned in the following verse of the *Gita*.

सर्वाणीन्द्रियकर्माणि प्राणकर्माणि चापरे ।

आत्मसंयमयोगाग्नौ जुह्वति ज्ञानदीपिते ॥

(Some again offer all the works of their senses and the
works of the vital force into the fire of the Yoga of self-
control, kindled by knowledge) (The *Gita*, IV, 27).

Arun Joshi's most recent novel, *The Last Labyrinth*, also
portrays this illusory world, which makes man "bewildered"
(The *Gita*, II, 72), as in a labyrinth in which the human soul
is lost in the criss-crossing pathways of countless desires
and sensuous pleasures :

इन्द्रियाणि मनो बुद्धिरस्याधिष्ठानमुच्यते ।

एतैर्विमोहयत्येष ज्ञानमावृत्य देहिनम् ॥

(The senses, the mind and the intelligence are said to be
its seat. Veiling wisdom by these, it deludes the embodied (soul) (The *Gita*, III, 40).

The protagonist Som Bhaskar bears a name which embodies the duality of his nature—what he is and what he wants
to be. 'Som' (the moon) may be said to stand for sensuous
pleasures and 'Bhaskar' (the sun) for the clear light of
faith.   He is tied by the bondage of desire :

"Beyond them all, audible only to my ear, a grey cry
threshed the night air : I want. I want. I want. Through

the light of my days and the blackness of my nights and the disquiet of those sleepless hours beside my wife, within reach of the tranquillisers, I had sung the same strident song : I want, I want. I want." (p. 11).

He seems, however, to have a higher overseeing self which realizes the vacuity of worldly wants and seems to push him towards the right direction. As he says to Aftab near the end of the novel.

"There is an understanding that only suffering and humiliation bring. Anuradha has that. Even I have a bit of it. You are empty of that understanding." (p. 217).

It seems that a part of him wants to achieve faith, to pray, to suffer from both hunger of the body and the hunger of the spirit (p. 11).

He confesses :

I knew that money was dirt, a whore. So were houses, cars, carpets. I knew of Krishna, of the lines he had spoken; of Buddha at Sarnath, under the full moon of July, setting in motion the wheel of Righteousness; of Pascal, on whom I did a paper at Harvard:

'Let us weigh the gain and loss in wagering that God is, let us estimate these two chances. If you gain, you gain all, if you lose, you lose nothing.' All this I knew and much else. And yet, at the age of thirtyfive, I could do no better than produce the same rusty cry : I want. I want (pp. 11-12).

He talks of "The First Cause" (p. 26) and of "the fundamental unity in the construction of the universe" (p. 27). Boating on the Ganga at Benaras he seems to transcend time and space : "I felt as though this was not Ganga but some unknown stream, in some unknown segment of the universe, leading to a reality that I had not yet known" (p. 49). At another time he realizes the littleness of man "like an ant threading through a maze, knocking about, against one wall, then another" (p. 53). Trying to analyze what he really wants, he speculates :

I want, I want. If only one knew what one wanted. Or, may be, to know was what I wanted. To know just that. No more. No less. This, then, was a labyrinth, too, this going forward and backward and sideways of the mind. I felt again the faint stirrings of a curiosity that I had first felt near the marble sarcophagus, a secret curiosity that I dare not share with another," (p. 53).

He is always haunted by "the spoken or unspoken question…what lay in the last labyrinth ?" (p. 122). He feels the need of "trust" (p. 63) and regards himself as a 'leper', that needed a cure (p. 126).

Som's cure is not far to seek. He seems to have a strong desire to conquer his lower self (The *Gita*, VI, 6) and to understand the mystery of the labyrinth of life and of the last labyrinth of death. He partially qualifies for God's Grace :

तमेव शरणं गच्छ सर्वभावेन भारत ।

तत्प्रसादात्परां शान्तिं स्थानं प्राप्स्यसि शाश्वतम् ।

[Flee unto Him for shelter with all thy being, O Bharata (Arjuna). By His grace shalt thou obtain supreme peace and eternal abode.] (The *Gita*, XVIII, 62).

Glimpses of the Lord's Grace are visible in the novel both in his craving for a higher vision of life and in the events that happen to him through the agency of characters who are the Lord's instruments : Anuradha, who bestows love and sympathy on him and saves him through a miracle from certain death of heart-attack; the old man, who travels nine hundred miles to die by the side of a certain lake; Gargi, who gives him the much sought-for controlling shares of Aftab's company and makes him realize the uselessness of worldly possessions; and, above all, his wife, Geeta, whose "trademark" is "trust" which Som needs (p. 63), and who at the end, saves him from committing the sin of suicide, rousing him as befits her name, from the sleep (तमोगुण), of ignorance. Som's raising his "weary palm" to her (p. 224) may be a gesture of understanding and acceptance. *The Last Labyrinth* seems to depict the vague but unmistakable reaching out for faith and understanding by a man lost in the labyrinth of desires and the vague simmerings of his discontent with this type of life. Som Bhaskar's lyrical cry to the presumably dead Anuradha

is similar to the prayers of saints and devotees like Tukaram mentioned by him. The Lord helps such creatures if
only they run towards him. Som Bhaskar's career illustrates the supreme message of the *Gita* :

सर्वधर्मान्परित्यज्य मामेक शरणं व्रज ।

अहं त्वा सर्वपापेभ्यो मोक्षयिष्यामि मा शुच: ।

(Abandoning all duties, come to Me alone for shelter.
Be not grieved, for I shall release thee from all evils.)
(The *Gita,* XVIII, 66).

The presence of Lord Krishna seems to loom large over
the novel—as one whom Anuradha worships, as one who
saves Som's life, as one who owns the controlling shares
in Aftab's company and as a mysterious flame in a remote
temple, a miniature of the Lord's refulgence described in
Chapter II of the *Gita. The Last Labyrinth* seems to lay stress
on "Sankhyayoga" as *The Foreigner* had done on "Karmayoga". Both lead to the same goal, the salvation of man.

The novels of Arun Joshi, thus, re-enact in modern contexts some of the important teachings and concepts of the
Gita, the relevance of which is everlasting. Lord Krishna
rightly asserts :

न त्वेवाहं जातु नासं न त्वं नेमे जनाधिपा: ।

न चैव न भविष्याम: सर्वे वयमत: परम् ।।

(Never was there a time when I was not, nor thou, nor
these lords of men, nor will there ever be a time hereafter when we shall cease to be) (The *Gita*, II, 12).

Radhakrishnan makes the meaning more explicit by explaining that the reference in this verse is to "the pre-exis-
tence and post-existence of the empirical egos". He goes
on to say, "Each individual is an ascent from initial non-
existence to full existence as a real, from *asat* to *sat*"[8]. One
can hardly describe better the attempts of Arun Joshi's
protagonists to transcend the "dark, mossy labyrinths of
the soul that languish forever, hidden from the dazzling
light of the sun"[9] and arrive at some sort of self-realiza-
tion and self-fulfilment. During this process they also
become aware of the depths of degradation to which man
can fall. One is conscious, in most of Arun Joshi's novels,
of the higher self of the protagonist scrutinizing and con-

demning the lower self and attempting to break loose from its shackles. As Colin Wilson has said, "so long as a man is not horrified at himself, he knows nothing about himself".[10] The two selves in Arun Joshi's fiction seem to come close to the description of "Kshetra" and the ' Kshestrajna" in the *Gita* :

इदं शरीरं कौन्तेय क्षेत्रमित्यभिधीयते ।
एतद्यो चेति तं प्राहुः क्षेत्रज्ञ इति तद्विदः ॥

(This body, O Son of Kunti (Arjuna), is called the field and him who knows this, those who know thereof call the knower of the field) (The *Gita*, XIII, 1).

Radhakrishnan's commentary brings out the relevance of these concepts to Joshi's novels : "man is a two-fold contradictory being, free and enslaved. He is godlike and has in him the signs of his fall, that is, descent into nature ..He appears to be actuated solely by elemental forces, sensual impulses, fear and anxiety. But man desires to get the better of his fallen nature."[11] This seems to sum up the essence of the dilemmas and quests of Arun Joshi's protagonists who realize that above this worldly glamour and materialistic progress there are higher and undefinable values. The soul of man, a bewildered foreigner in this deluding world of the senses, should become a true apprentice of the Lord and by right action, penance, harking back to the call of the primordial, or attaining knowledge of oneself by constant self-scrutiny, thread through the labyrinth of life and the last labyrinth of death reaching the right affirmations and ultimate salvation. Arun Joshi thinks that *The Foreigner* and *The Strange Case of Billy Biswas*" are primarily concerned with religious issues—the problems of an essentially Hindu mind."[12] This statement is true, in varying degrees and in different ways, of all his novels, which seem to enshrine or occasionally point to some of the teachings of the *Gita*. In this age of soulless technology and hollow rationalism it is necessary to remember that, their parameters defined, they should be transcended into faith as Anuradha in *The Last Labyrinth* puts it so clearly : "Maybe Krishna begins where Darwin left off."[13]

REFERENCES

1. S. Radhakrishnan. *Cur Heritage* (New Delhi : Orient Paperbacks, 1973), pp 44-45.
2. Sujatha Mathai, "I'm a Stranger to my Books", *The Times of India*, July 7, 1983, p. 8. Quoted by Thakur Guru Prasad in "The Lost Lonely Questers of Arun Joshi's Fiction", in R.K. Dhawan (ed.), *The Fictional World of Arun Joshi* (New Delhi : Classical Publishing Company, 1986), p. 155.
3. Arun Joshi, *The Foreigner*, (Delhi: Hind Pocket Books, rpt. 1972), p. 80. All subsequent references to this work have been absorbed in the text without repeating the title.
4. S. Radhakrishnan. *The Bhagavadgita* (London: George Allen and Unwin, 1948; rpt, 1949). Chapter VI Verse 1. All subsequent English translations of the verses of the *Gita* and quotations from S. Radhakrishnan's Commentary are from this book.
5. *Ibid.*, p. 230.
6. R.S. Pathak, "Human Predicament and Meaninglessness in Arun Joshi's Novels", in Dhawan (ed,) *op. cit.*, pp. 132-33.
7. Arun Joshi, *The Apprentice* (New Delhi : Orient Paperbacks, 1974), p. 149. All subsequent references to this work have been absorbed in the text without repeating the title.
8. S. Radhakrishnan, *op. cit.*, p. 103.
9. Arun Joshi, *The Srange Case of Billy Biswas* (New Delhi : Orient Paperbacks, 1971), p. 8.
10. Colin Wilson, *The Outsider* (London : Pan Books, 1956), p. 316.
11. Radhakrishnan, *op. cit,*, p. 301.
12. Arun Joshi's reply to M.R. Dua, quoted in Dhawan (ed.), *op. cit.*, p. 20.
13. Arun Joshi, *The Last Labyrinth* (New Delhi : Orient Paperbacks, 1981), p. 132.

14

Shashi Deshpande's If I Die Today: A Meistic Analysis

A. K. AWASTHI

Meism is a philosophy that aims at the achievement of total individuality within the individual-self realising its essential ME through its thought and action culminating in a state of negation of self-consciousness, self-assertive approach to self (a state of resonance with regard to the knowledge of the real self) without destroying the social basis of the individual by desocializing the individual and thus redeeming the society of its autocratic, arbitrary socialization of individual action. It promotes an attitude to life which prompts an individual to live according to his or her need and thus gain the real self before he or she could gain the other-self or become true to it. In the present study an effort has been made to interpret as well as analyse human sensibility in terms of meistic approach to life.

Close on the heels of Anita Desai, Shashi Deshpande is emerging fast as a potential novelist writing in English. She began her literary career as a short story writer in English in 1975. Five years later her competence as a novelist was noticed when she produced three novels in quick succession : *The Dark Holds No Terrors* (*1980*), *If I Die Today* (*1982*) and *Come Up And Be Dead* (*1983*)—so far her last. In all the three novels she has shown a keen insight into human psychology. She has made an effort to probe the self-psychosis of man. In selection of subject matter, technique of writing and thematic pattern, she has shown an anti-traditional attitude towards the craft of fiction. She is concerned with the roots of the sickness of today. As O'Neill once put it, "We must dig at the roots of the sickness of today", Deshpande digs deeper into the earthly nature of human relationship in order to excavate the known but seldom understood principles of life, which might help individuals to live happily and successfully.

II

According to Shashi Deshpande man lives under various kinds of pressures or tensions. He is virtually over-ridden with these. The obvious situation leads to a point of no return. It culminates in an irrevocable illusion of living, beyond which there is no escape. So he is rather condemned to live under illusion, which he has to consider to be a happy situation sometimes knowingly and other times being oblivious of the facts of life. The result is a stalemate in thinking process. The much wanted harmony between thought and action is not only disrupted but a clear vision of life also becomes a far cry.

The novelist illustrates the situation vividly. The thematic pattern shows her craftsmanship in modes of treatment, viz. man and his own self, man and Nature, which however, overlap constantly. She operates on the unconscious level of human sensibility. She finds that the basic desire of man to be first himself is scuttled amidst the humdrum and hullabaloo of life. He is so intensely overswayed by other considerations, that, even though he knows and wants to be true to himself, he lets almost all opportunities slip from him before it becomes too late to realize what he essentially is and what for he has been living so far. That, what he wanted, was clear and unclouded, but it never occurred to him clearer than now. Thus, man thwarts his own ambitions and self. Yet he repents but without remorse for the illusion that has been his very life and that is still a dominant notion with him. He is helpless; he cannot disbelieve that he believed the disbelievable. This is a paradox of life and he knows it. And yet he is unable to muster up courage to come out of his shell to throw away the garb of hypocrisy and be his real self. So he is doomed to be perhaps what he has to be. Nature has made him function like that. He believes that he had to be somebody else not knowing that he has become what he had to be.

The essence of this paradox of life is his own fear to face himself. If he learns to do that, he will have 'the feel of a real man'in himself; he is likely to be his own ME within and without. But on account of that illusory happiness, he is unable to realise this simple truth. So he frets and fumes, laughs and weeps, does and meets evil, goes on mechanically in a rut of life scarcely asserting his own will (ME). As the novelist begins with doubt, she is scientific in her approach. Then she reasons with herself just to emphasize the process of self-analysis and assessment. She observes life and its surroundings detachedly and reports objectively. Apparently her prime concern is Death, its nature and implication, and why do we fear it? But, in fact, she is trying to analyse human existence— whether it is real or unreal.

III

To Shashi Deshpande life is real but it has been corrupted by want of self-assessment — a human weakness. This view finds expression in *If I Die Today*, in which she deals with a sense of violence around people as the motif. Manju is the narrator of the story. Whatever she says is either supported or reanimated by Guru, who is the pivotal character in the novel. Conceptually they speak the same philosophy in different aspects. In fact, it is a matter of one's vision, how far it goes. Manju thinks that the birth of her child is a 'cosmic accident' ; Guru elaborates the statement," (but) it is not merely a meaningless accident. There is instead always a meaning, a coherence, only if you look for it ... the pity is, one realises this too late."[1] This is what may be considered to be Deshpande's probing into self. However, during discussion on the subject Manju sounds like an existentialist when she seemingly contradicts Guru's viewpoint ; "Birth, life on the whole is a meaningless accident" and that there is "no past, no future, just that one exquisitely happpy moment", i.e. the present.[2] But, thereafter she laments her own weakness as Guru points out that she does not possess the personality like that of an innocent child, "so open and unguarded", therefore she is not true to her own self. She knows it but has almost no willingness to be herself before being any other. And this is the core of the whole problem of unbalanced outlook to life which is a sequel to the development of a distorted and self-contradictory personality.

Comparing herself with Meera (it is also applicable to man/woman in general) she says that "it was her manner, spontaneous and direct, no evasions. While I ... With Meera, anything that isn't glorious is a catastrophe. There are no in betweens. Therefore, she positively enjoys being a wife, mother, housekeeper, cook and all that it involves, i.e. the present."[3] Meera possesses a natural behaviour while Manju or any other man or woman doesn't. The other side of the picture dipicts Guru as horribly frank and open about things, "rather an infantile terrible in company. Pretences, even polite social ones had no place in his life (p.8)". Perhaps the novelist would wish people to observe Guru as he approaches others directly as a human being. This is of course the most forceful aspect of his personality that impressed all at once ; "That, I think, was what made all of us succumb to him finally," said Manju (p.8). Since he suffers from cancer, he is to die soon still he is a brave man "who (has) risen above all human weakness and crossed that dreadful barrier ... the eternal fear of death" (p.9). This quality makes Guru more fearless and more objective than others who recoil into their illusion and call his free and unprejudiced observation dangerous, even incriminating and also an abject interference in their 'peaceful' lives, however, shadowed by illusion confused with happiness, for constant knowledge of what is illusion becomes a source of tension for such persons, The tragedy with these people is 'that they lack the will to be free and observant; that is why they suffer, whereas Guru understands it. He, therefore, plans to do something, within whatever time is left, starting with the present moment. For he can't "leave anything to the vague future" (p.9). There is seemingly a contradiction between his belief and saying. Planning is always a futuristic term. If he plans, he believes in Future, yet he says, he doesn't. Perhaps as he has the knowledge that very little time is left with him, his knowledge becomes the part of the present. So there is no real contradiction in his thought. To him 'tomorrow' is not a fact but a continuous present ; it is a phenomenal situation to which we have to give a name. He is consistent in his approach to life as Manju says, "It seems to me that Guru had begun to see himself as a spectator, above and different from all of us. That's when a man becomes dangerous, yes, dangerous because he imagines himself to be God and loses touch with humanity (p.9). This is an ironical statement ; he is a danger to those who are not natural in their behaviour.

As a matter of fact, there is always a danger to those who fear to be exposed to themselves, what they really are. They wish to remain in their illusory world of evasive happiness and don't want any interference therein. It is a different thing that, as Meera says, "May be, he just showed us up for what we really were. So tension took all but Guru in its grip" (p. 9), for they had been made aware of the reality; still they dared not wish to come out of their old selves. All this assessment of the protagonist's personality implies that he seems to be speaking like an existentialist but behaves differently, i.e. like a meist who indulges in a self-conscious, self-assertive pursuit of self that differentiates between the individual self, i.e.' Me' and the Ultimate self, i.e. 'I'.

The situation about others would have been different if awareness had dawned upon them. Had they become meistic in approach to life like Guru, there would have been no tension. Instead they would have enjoyed the present moment without ever bothering for the future or thinking of the past. Above all man needs a confidence in himself and the present. Guru possesses this quality. He knows that doctors keep on saying to a dying man. 'You're all right, until you die" (p. 11). Guru knows this so he has neither illusions nor expectations, neither worry nor remorse; he is happy and direct to everything. Man knows that he can't control life, though he lives under the illusion that he can. But, when things start slipping out of his hands, he resents it and becomes sorrowful on getting failure for certain. It is at this point that the natural man within him assumes the lead of personality. He uses force to retain what he is going to lose or has lost already. In this way violence carves out a place for itself in man's tension-ridden mind and which sooner or later becomes the most dominant aspect of his personality. Thus, violence takes its roots not in the outside world but in thought of man.

The novelist emphasizes that man does not want to overcome his malady. He does not want to face the knowledge that he is going to lose everything one day, that he will die. The only difference is that if others die today, he'll die tomorrow or vice versa. Still he doesn't like things going out of his control. He knows, he can't control life and its course of events despite his best efforts and also his being future-conscious. So, what is the harm if one learns to behave as naturally as Meera does even in other people's homes : "Meera was one of those persons who behave as naturally in other people's homes as they do in their own." (p. 18). But Manju illustrates that man is bent upon evading the reality. Taking trifles as the fundamental situation he imposes upon himself a happy illusion that he controls his own life and that there is no fate whatsoever; if he wants to drink hot coffee, he will, there is none to stop him : "No, there is no fate, Meera, there's only us. And we can control our own life. See, you can drink hot coffee, if you want to. I've proved it," said Manju,

(p. 20). However, this is no argument. There may or may not be any fate but there are many things which are beyond his control. One thing cannot be the basis of any gene- ralization about the whole. A trifle is no substitute to pro- blems of life beyond our control. Manju says: "It's easy to make surmises now. For may be the real truth is that it was just a statement that ended up as a joke..." (p. 20). And man jokes with himself throughout his life. He has been doing so ever since he discovered his faculty of reasoning. He abandoned his true self and imposed upon himself a non-truth as truth ; for he found his real self awfully truthful. In fact, he had no courage to face his own self.

IV

So it is the fear-self, that is ultimately reflected in each man's fear of death. A life rooted in fear leads to various kinds of fear. He fears from everything. As he possesses an illusion of happiness, he fears its exposure ; he con- siders his material gains as real achievement and fears to lose them. Then there are also other people who wish to gain material wealth by fair or foul means. Thus, two types of mentality evolve—the fearsome and the fearing. Nobody wishes to lose his possessions, perhaps never, so he doesn't want to die for he'll lose everything. He is not concerned that even if he gains the world, he loses his soul. So he fears death. Probably this is the reason why man resorts to violence; whenever there is the least appre- hension of losing something. It may be violence in thought, words, or deeds with which he hopes to restrict his adversary and thereby retain or consolidate his mate- rial gains. This is how violence becomes part of his per- sonality. Any act done towards the enlargement of his personality leads to what is called sin. The personality developed in this area has two purposes : primarily to overawe others that they might not even think of distur- bing one's gains and secondly, to nurture one's own illu- sion of happiness through material gains by rigorously following the policy of aggrandisement. Yet this is not all. To the question why does man wish to possess anything, the answer is 'it is his natural instinct'. It implies that violence, which is rooted in personality, is the result of natural phenomenon. Moreover, we also find violence to be the dominant principle of Nature. The seed sprouts by doing violence to its mother-body which is destroyed in the process. The same principle is seen in everything everywhere. The sense of possession in human relationship also leads to violence, whether it be the question of dealing with a child or loving the spouse. Violence, therefore, is a natural principle which remains with man to allow him to survive. Perhaps there is no getting away from it. Still man has the option to allow or not to allow his being to be subjected to the fear-psychosis which culminates in violence. It is this sense of violence around people that Shashi Deshpande has dealt with in the novel.

The novelist operates on two levels : notional and physical. She examines a great psychological question, how and why man is prone to sinister deeds. She finds that since life is rooted in violence, it is fraught with pain and misery. But the notion of violence is not negative in character. On the contrary it is positive element of life. She, therefore, differs from most of her predecessors and contemporaries in treating violence with sympathy and positiveness. She regards it is an essential factor in life, so it is justified. Vidya, who kills Tony and Guru and makes an unsuccessful attempt on the life of Vijay is declared in the end a psychic case rather than a criminal. The two levels of violence are clearly projected through relationship combinations, viz. Manju and Vijay, Tony and Cynthia, Kulkarni, and his daughter, Mriga, Vidya and Vijay, Vidya and her brother, Manju and her daughter. Through these relationships Deshpande highlights the sense of violence around people. It is part of our natural self. It will remain with us so long as we do not abjure (the tendency) our lust to play loose and fast with our own self and the same we can't do for we are reluctant by our nature as Nature has divested us with conflicting elemental forces ; it has crippled our ingenuity and thrown a challenge to balance ourselves in view of such basic oddities of life. Thus, poor man has fallen a victim to his own self, own doubts and disbeliefs. He gropes in the dark to find a way but finally his efforts end up in smoke. Scarcely one rises to the occasion and stimulates the challenge successfully but his experience is so microcosmic in kind that it hardly acquires the leverage to impress the people. His experience vanishes with him, or else he is deified, i.e. put on the wrong gear. He is adored but seldom understood and the life of man drifts slowly towards an unbidding end.

It may be argued that since violence is a natural principle, should all violence be justified ? For this we have to keep in mind that natural violence has a purpose. It is always for creation. If it appears to be for destruction, then it destroys only what has become unproductive and useless, which will be replaced by the new forces of creation. The same principle applies also to distorted forms of expression. But as the most ferocious animals and turbulent streams can be tamed to some extent, similarly violence in man's nature can be curbed to a considerable extent ; man is intelligent enough to understand it. Then, if he is able to shun fear altogether, he can successfully do away with violence as part of his personality. He would not forget violence ; he would have it but only as an attribute and not as an element dominating his personality. He would remain truly natural shunning fear as a result of his awareness of his own ME and also having violence as an attribute to be aroused on purpose. In this way he would be free from psychosis. His ME having realized its real self would assert in a self-conscious manner.

REFERENCES

1. Shashi Deshpande, *If I Die Today*, Ghaziabad : Vikas Publishing House, 1982, pp. 10-11.
2. *Ibid.,* p. 4.
3. *Ibid.,* p. 5.

15

Salman Rushdie's Treatment of Alienation

R. S. PATHAK

Salman Rushdie has established himself as one of the most provocative modern writers. With just four novels – *Grimus* (1975), *Midnight's Children* (1980), *Shame* (1983) and *The Satanic Verses* (1988) – to his credit, he has been recognized as a major novelist delineating the contemporary scene on the Indian subcontinent. Few novels in recent years have unleashed so much praise and criticism as *Midnight's Children* did when it won the coveted Booker McConnell Award for 1981. According to a reviewer, "it is a very un-Indian book about things Indian", which presents "a wonderful mix of the beautiful and the grotesque that... only India seems to offer to the Western world."[1] The novel earned unqualified praise from the *New York Times* which held that Rushdie's masterpiece 'sounds like a continent finding its voice.' Rushdie's other novels also display, in their own ways, his achievements and limitations as a novelist.

Rushdie has called himself 'a fairly political animal.'[2] All his novels except the first, which is ahistorical, have dealt with historical/political themes. Commenting on *Midnight's Children* and *Shame*, Rushdie told an interviewer : "It seems to me that everything in both books has had to do with politics and with the relationship of the individuals and history".[3] His novels are, however, something

more than historical/political accounts of certain individuals' experiences and reactions. What imparts real significance to them is his intense awareness of the predicament
of the modern man. As M. K. Naik points out, 'Midnight's
Children...illustrates the permanent plight of individual
identity in the hostile modern world.'[4] This is true of all
his novels except Grimus. The novelist has portrayed in
considerable depth the dilemma of the alienated person.
"Such angst. Such loneliness. Such rootlessness," ex-
claims Dilip Fernandez after going through Rushdie's novels,
and adds : "But this is the stuff creation is made of" in
the modern world.[5] Unlike historical/political issues, the
problems treated in Rushdie's novels are of perennial interest, and it would be interesting to see how he presents
the essential predicament of the modern man.

The impact of alienation on the modern man has been
corrosive. It can be seen today in its various manifestations, the most conspicuous being : generation gap, com-
partmentalization of life resulting in schizophrenia, chopp-
ing off of human relationships and concerns, personal crises
culminating in stunting of personal development, and so
on. Twentieth century—especially the post-war period—
has been a period of great spiritual and mental stress and
strain, and has rightly been called 'The Age of Alienation.'[6] The modern man finds himself in a particularly
inhospitable world. As Edmund Fuller suggests, in our
age "man suffers not only from war, persecution, famine
and ruin, but from inner problem...a conviction of isolation, randomness, [and] meaninglessness in his very existence."[7] Rushdie's novels have faithfully delineated this
very plight of the contemporary society.

The modern man's sense of alienation gets aggravated
by his lack of faith and abundance of uncertainty. Diag-
nosing the malaise, Paul Brunton aptly remarks : "Never
before were so many people plunged in so much uncertainty, so much perplexity and unsettlement."[8] The plight
of the modern man has been discussed by Melvin Seeman
under a set of five interrelated operational conditions, viz.
powerlessness, normlessness, isolation, self-estrange--

ment and meaninglessness.[9] These are, in fact, different manifestations of alienation. Taviss subsumes them under two kinds, i.e. 'social alienation' and self-aliena-tion.'[10] In Rushdie's novels we come across both the forms of alienation.

For historical reasons, Indian writers in English are particularly susceptible to rootlessness. It is really diffi-cult to specify the precise nature of alienation depicted in Indian fiction in English. "It would be interesting", how-ever, as Melwani points out. ''...to examine how far 'root-lessness' is a deep-seated malady, how far a fad and how far a posture. The attempts made so far to portray the effects of Westernization are either intellectual, farcical or philosophical. What is required is a portrayal ina rtistic terms.'[11] The present paper aims at analysing Rushdie's treatment of alienation from this very point of view.

II

Rushdie's first novel, *Grimus*, is replete with hallu-cinogenic intensity. Flapping Eagle, the hero of the tale, swallows the elixir of immortality and wanders the face of the earth for over seven centuries. He sees things 'most men miss in a mere lifetime.' But before he reaches the town of K in the mythical world of Calf island, he suffers the onslaught of the 'inner dimensions'. He journeys up a mountain where he eventually encounters Grimus. (Grimus is, incidentally, an anagram of Simurg, in Persian mythology the bird with reasoning powers).

Superficially, Flapping Eagle seems [to have adapta-bility and capacity to make compromises. But he almost invariably gets "reduced to the status of a pawn in some-one else's game."[12] Flapping Eagle is ostracized from his tribe because of his ambiguous sex, his birth and pig-mentation. 'Long estranged', he develops a 'rarefied, abstract attitude to life' (p. 269). He comes to realize in due course that his quest has been 'A gigantic blind alley. A voyage through the waste land' (p. 90). Fre-quently haunted by 'the weight of his guilt' and 'the feel-

ing of futility', on account of which 'his morale had been
steadily declining', he feels like 'an empty man, a Shell
without a Form' (p. 205).

What tortures Flapping Eagle most is the overwhelming
'contrariness' of things. He is filled with an intense desire
to get to the bottom of contradictions and anomalies of
life (p. 157). His efforts to decipher the meaning of
life are, however, thwarted on various occasions, and he
remains 'chameleon, adaptable, confused' (p. 249). We
are pertinently told :

> To have been so much and done so little. Searching,
> always searching for the path through the maize... . It
> had left him half a man, unfound even by himself. It
> was this lack in himself that was now reaching a time of
> crisis (p. 90).

The fate of Virgil Jones, another important character in
the novel, has not been very different from that of Flapping Eagle. Jones's struggle in life has 'drained him of a
great deal more than energy', and he appears to Flapping
Eagle as a 'shambling, bumbling, ineffectual' being
(p. 100). Jones is, as he himself knows, 'a stranger' within
himself (p. 123). He wouldn't see any sense in living
'the same day over and over again' ; only 'displaced persons' are 'always counterfeiting roots' (p. 87). Ultimately,
Jones ceases to see the merit in achievement or heroism
(p. 45). He also tends to be somewhat conservative
and unadventurous. The urge to fit in has taken over and
the spirit of adventure and the passion for long-time search
has waned in him (p. 128). He sums up his experiences
of life in the following words :

> Unfortunately life has a way of sidetracking one's
> greatest ambitions. Painters, would-be artists, end up
> whitewashing walls. Sculptors are forced to design
> toilets. Writers become critics or publicists. [And]
> Archaeologists...can become gravediggers (p. 44).

This pathetic condition is bound to generate alienation
of an acute nature. Rushdie's next two novels have taken
up this theme for fuller treatment.

III

Rushdie's masterpiece, *Midnight's Children*, is a novel about Indian independence and the partition and its aftermath. It contains the novelist's interpretation of a period of about seventy years in India's modern history. In writing this novel, Rushdie's "aim was to relate private lives to public events and to explore the limits of individuality in a country as big, as populous and as culturally variegated as India."[13] *Midnight's Children* encapsulates the experiences of three generations of the Sinai family, living in Srinagar, Amritsar and Agra and then in Bombay and, finally, migrating to Karachi. Alongside of the collective history of a nation, we have personal experiences of the narrator, Saleem Sinai.

As Keith Wilson has pointed out, *Midnight's Children* is 'the novel of national angst.'[14] Right from the beginning, Saleem is conscious of his historical 'centrality', his destiny being 'indissolubly chained' to that of his country. He is fully convinced that his birth at 'the benighted moment' thrust upon him 'at the best of times a dangerous sort of involvement'.[15] He fails to understand, however, the reason for having being born, which always remains 'shadowy still, undefined, [and] enigmatic' (p. 193). He remembers himself as 'a lonely ugly child' (p. 240). He has no doubts whatsoever that he is doomed to lead the life of an exile :

> At every turn I am thwarted, a prophet in the wilderness, like Maslama, like ibn Sinan ; No matter how I try, the desert is my lot (p. 471).

In his bravado, Saleem assumes upon himself the self-styled role of a prophet, which may be a highly questionable issue. But one thing is certain : he has to lead the life of a social outcast. Throughout his life, he remains 'adrift in this haze of anticipation' of a better life (p. 180). But till the end he remains 'consigned to the peripheries of history' (p. 470). He is ultimately flattened like the ancestral spitoon by forces beyond his control.

Saleem confesses to have developed uneasy symptoms of schizophrenia (p. 420). He says :

I admit openly I have not been myself of late. I have been a buddha, and a basketed ghost, and a would-be-Saviour of the nation...rushing down blind alleys,... [with] considerable problems with reality (p. 520).

He is nevertheless obsessed with the purpose of life. It was at a very early age that he became "perplexed by meaning" (p. 181). "Everything has shape, if you look for it," he says. "There is no escape from form" (p. 271). His is, however, a frustrated search for meaning or pattern in life, and he does not possess a clear sense of purpose :

I became afraid that everything was wrong — that my much trumpeted existence might turn out to be utterly useless, void, and without the shred of a purpose (p. 180).

Saleem variegated experiences are such that they only make him 'always confused about being good' (p. 239). He neither acquires a philosophical wisdom, like that of a prophet, nor does he understand the commonsense solution to life's problems, like the one suggested by his counter ego, Shiva : "You got to get what you can, do what you can with it, and then you got to die" (p. 264). In this respect, Saleem's lot is typical of all alienated persons. He himself admits : I am "so far gone, in my desperate need for meaning, that I'm prepared to distort everything...in my confusion I can't judge" (p. 198). This confusion turns out to be the besetting sin of Saleem's sensibility and conduct.

Saleem betrays at times characteristics of an 'anti-hero'. He had 'acquired a miraculous gift', but chooses to 'conceal his talents'. This is so not because of any humility but because of an abysmal self-estrangement. He fritters away his remarkable talents 'on inconsequential voyeurism and petty cheating' (p. 204). He is not even clear about his place in the scheme of things and finds himself 'elusive as rainbows, unpredictable as lightning, [and] garrulous as Ganesh' (p. 234). He remains all along 'an unfortunate fellow with a face like a cartoon', fatally 'gripped by some deep malaise' (p. 385).

Saleem's self-estrangement is partly the outcome of his abnormally morbid nature and partly of his nurture and inheritance. The Reverend Mother, we are told, led a lonely life 'like a large smug spider' (p. 41). The whole household was very often torn by the conflict between grand-paternal scepticism and grandmaternal credulity (p. 124). Saleem's father was 'unnerved, adrift, unmanned' (p. 397). Similarly, his mother became the victim of the 'spirit of detached fatigue' (p. 393) and, in due course, 'fell apart' (p. 393). Saleem's sister Jamila, too, despite her faith and vocation, was not really different from the other members of her family. Like them, she was filled with 'the pain of exile' and 'the lovelessness of life' (p. 472). Saleem himself suffers from a strange weariness—'a general fatigue so profound' (p. 391) that he becomes 'adrift, disorientated' (p. 389). A time comes when he forgets even his name, which is the most significant emblem of one's identity. In the hostile world he is flung to live, he feels that he is 'cast as a ghost' (p. 29). He particularly draws attention to his pathetic condition :

> Please believe that I am falling apart . . . . I mean quite simply that I have begun to crack all over like an old jug . . . . In short, I am literally disintegrating, slowly for the moment, although there are signs of an acceleration (p. 37).

Saleem is constantly haunted by his 'special doom', which he finds 'impossible to ignore' (p. 143). "I am empty and free", he reiterates (pp. 409-10). He feels that he is "pulled up by his roots to be flung unceremoniously across the years, [and] fated to plunge memoryless into an adulthood whose every aspect grew daily more grotesque" (p. 414). Towards the close of the novel he comes to realise that he will have to 'jerk towards my crisis like a puppet with broken strings' (p. 509). Saleem's is thus the predicament of an alienated person.

In *Midnight's Children* the novelist has taken special pains to thrash the issue of Saleem Sinai's identity and his predicament in a hostile world. The protagonist's identity, as revealed in the novel, is shown as fractured and fragmented and merged and superimposed. His incurable sterility makes his case particularly pathetic. His plight has been suggested in various ways. The two important parameters are Saleem's personal appearance and his heredity, both of which have been particularly highlighted by the novelist.

There is something uncanny about Saleem's personal appearance. As he himself tells us, his 'large moon-face was too large : too perfectly round' (p. 124). This is worsened by 'something lacking in the region of the chin' (p. 124). Both these features as symptomatic of his lack of will power and barrenness. That Saleem is not all a piece is indicated by certain glaring physical details. The birthmarks 'spread down my western hairline, a dark patch coloured my eastern ear', the 'rampant cucumber of the nose' and 'temples like stunted horns' (p. 124) indicate lack of harmony in his face and personality and also his being reduced to animal level. His unblinking eyes and legs that were irretrievably bowed' (p. 149) are also expressive of his passive and unstable nature.

As for his heredity, Saleem himself confides, he 'had more mothers than most mothers have children' (p. 243). 'All my life,' he further says, "consciously, or unconsciously I have sought out fathers' (p. 426), and 'giving birth to parents has been one of my stranger talents' (p. 243). Besides his real mother Vanita and his putative mother Amina, the midwife Mary Pereira, who performed baby-swapping and gave a new life to Saleem, was a kind of mother to him. In due course of time, he was entrusted to the care of his aunt Pia and was thus 'promoted to occupy the sacred place of the son she never had' (p. 243). Saleem's 'fathers' outnumber his 'mothers'. The "mischievous perversity" of a dream "confused Amina about the parentage of her child" and "the child of midnight" was given "a fourth father [Nadir Khan] to set baside Winkie and Methwold and Ahmed Sinai" (pp. 127-28). The German 'snakedoctor' and his uncle General Zulfikar gave new lease of life to him. And the snake-charmer Picture Singh, who rescued him from Bangladesh, was 'the last in the line of men who have been willing to become my fathers' (p. 378). This state of affairs eloquently testifies to Saleem's lack of roots and identity crisis. Like his father, he himself had, metaphorically speaking, a 'brittle' life.

The motif of fragmentation is present throughout the novel. But in no case is it so prominent as it is in the case of Saleem. He is fully aware of his problems and plights, misfortunes and discordances, so typical of a rootless person. This is how he looks at himself finally :

> I'm tearing myself apart, can't even agree with myself, talking arguing like a wild fellow, cracking up, memory going, yes, memory plunging into chasms and being swallowed by the dark, only fragments remain, none of it makes sense any more (p. 503).

This is the height of self-alienation. This represents, in brief, the plight of Saleem's 'clock-ridden, crime-stained birth' (p. 4).

IV

Rushdie's third novel, *Shame*, depicts the contemporary political situation in Pakistan. The main plot of the novel revolves round the lives of Omar Khayyam Shakil and Sufiya Zenobia. The side-plot, however, involves relationships between two important architects of Pakistan—Raza Hyder and Iskander Harappa (who are, in fact, based on General Zia and Zulfikar Ali Bhutto respectively). Much of the novel is, as Rushdie himself suggests, "all about careerism, cops, politics, revenge, assassinations, executions, blood and guts".[16] But the novelist's portrayal of the psychological crisis of some of his characters is of no less interest.

Rushdie makes it a point to tell us that the society in Pakistan is, by and large, repressive – "a society which is authoritarian in its social and sexual codes, which crushes its women beneath the intolerable burdens of honour and propriety".[17] Iskander Harappa once told his daughter : "As a nation we have a positive genius for self-destruction, we nibble away at ourselves, we eat our children, we pull down anyone who climbs up" (p. 184). It is against a background like this that characters like Sufiya Zenobia and Omar Khayyam Shakil act and react.

Rushdie has shown how shame (i.e. *sharam*) is a part of 'the architecture of the society that the novel des-cribes'.[18] Many people in countries like Pakistan, he points out, grow upon 'a diet of honour and shame' (p. 115). "But shame is like everything else; live with it for long enough and it becomes part of the furniture" (p. 28). Angular persons like Sufiya are typical products of an unfortunate cultural climate like this, in which—

> Shameful things are done : lies, loose living, disres-pect for one's elders, failure to love one's national flag, incorrect voting at elections, over-eating, extramarital sex, autobiographical novels, cheating at cards, mal-treatment of womenfolk, examination failures, smuggl-ing, throwing one's wicket away at the crucial point of a Test Match : and they are done *Shamelessly* (p. 122).

Sufiya's violence may seem to be blind and pointless. It illustrates, however, a well-known historical truth about individual and social alienation. At times she symbolises mob violence, 'a rumour, a chimaera, the collective phan-tasy of a stifled people, a dream born of their rage' (p. 263). Rushdie establishes an unmistakable connec-tion between shame and violence. He writes : "If you push people too far and if you humiliate them too greatly, then a kind of violence bursts out of them". Sufiya's bes-tiality is nothing but an outrageous expression of her im-potent rage arising from her estrangement. Omar Khayyam, moved by her pathetic condition, wonders : "Can it be possible ... that human beings are capable of discovering their nobility in their savagery ?" (p. 254). There is, however, nothing really noble about her.

Sufiya has been described in the novel as 'the wrong miracle' (p. 89). She is so thoroughly self-estranged that her "body's defence mechanisms have declared war against the very life they are supposed to be protecting" (p. 142). An external manifestation of her psychic problems can be seen in her tendancy of having 'blushes like petrol fires' (p. 121). Her brain-fever enables her 'to absorb, like a sponge, a host of unfelt feelings' (p. 122). Sufiya's psychological problems have made her so uncontrollable that she is compared by Iskander Harappa to 'an impetuous river' which can not only inundate the plains but also cast down trees and buildings (p. 256).

Omar Khayyam Shakil's case is even more complicated' His lot is similar to that of the man who has ''lost his way completely'' and runs ''wildly about like a time-traveller who has lost his magic capsule and fears he will never emerge'' (p. 31). Shakil seems to have come to this world at a wrong time, descending upon 'the cohorts of history like a wolf (or a wolf-child) on the fold' (pp. 32-33). It is his 'distressed psychological condition' that makes him 'the victim of mental disorder' (p. 143). As he grows along, his alienation from his society and his self becomes all the more unmitigable.

It may be remembered that right from his early days Shakil was afflicted by 'a sense of inversion, of a world turned upside down' (p. 21). Trapped inside a 'reclusive mansion' and suffocated by his mothers' 'three-in-oneness', he grew into 'a spoiled and vulpine brat.' Having no illusions about his childhood, Shakil remembers it 'as a lover, abandoned, remembers his beloved' (p. 40). Even during his dreams, he plunges into the void and is reminded of his worthlessness (p. 22). The novelist has particularly emphasized his 'unstable wilderness', informing us that he ''grew up between twin eternities, whose conventional order was, in his experience, precisely inverted'' (p. 23). Like Saleem of *Midnight's Children*, Shakil was very often plagued by his 'sense of being a creature of the edge—a peripheral man' (p. 24). Painfully conscious of his ''congenitally isolated self'', he once described himself as ''a fellow who is not even the hero of his own life ; a man born and raised in the condition of being out of things'' (pp. 25, 24). In the town of Q., Shakil always finds himself 'an outsider' and 'homeless' (p. 47). For his uncanny personal habits, he is accused of 'being ugly inside as well as out, a Beast' (p. 144). Persons like Omar Khayyam, we are reminded, are 'monsters in a civilized society' and are condemned to walk on the 'uttermost rim' of the earth (p. 199). Summing up his impressions about Shakil, the novelist writes : 'I am no less disappointed in my hero than I was' (p. 198). Much of this dissatisfaction may be due to his protagonist's incurable alienation and its repercussions.

It may also not be inappropriate to remember that some other characters in the novel also suffer on account of their self-estrangement, thanks to their 'dislocated, rootless' country (p. 81) and 'the bizarre atmosphere of that horrified and dislocated time' (p. 169). Most people in such a context are 'falling away ...like rocket stages' (p. 238), and find it very difficult to 'emerge from the rubble of their exploded identity' (p. 38). Shakil's mothers are nothing less than 'psychological centaurs, fish-women, hybrid', affected severely by a 'confused separation of personalities' (p. 40). Even Raza Hyder does not fare significantly better. Initially, he appears to have 'a boulder-like quality'—'an indeflectible sense of himself' (p. 67). Later on, however, his self-control gives way and he begins to feel 'around him the enclosing emptiness of the void' (p. 238). He realizes, although a little too late, that the years of his glory 'had been no more than self-delusory lies' (p. 257). Raza's wife, Bilquis, is even more rootless. Despite her show of queenly composure, she behaves ''as though she were standing on a crumbling outcrop over an abyss'' (p. 103). She is ultimately reduced to 'less than a character, a mirage, almost a mumble in the corners of the palace' (p. 209). Sufiya, Shakil, Raza and Bilquis— all are victims of the same malaise, which manifests in each case in a different form and assumes varying proportions.

V

Alienation, as Meenakshi Mukherjee rightly points out, is 'a very common theme' in Indian Fiction in English.[19] Rushdie's alienated characters convey, in varying degrees, a sense of unhappy frustration resulting mainly from their social milieu. He has ruthlessly presented their social tragedy and psychological trauma. He wields irony and satire with competence, and his command over language enables him to depict crucial events and character-traits without melodrama. His treatment of ths rootless person's problems and plights keeps on becoming complex from novel to novel. So comprehensive and sure is his grasp over the psyche of his characters and social forces shaping them that a reviewer of *Midnight's Children* has maintained that "India has found her Günter Grass". Rushdie has also been compared to Milan Kundera and Gabriel Garcia Marquez.

As a creative historian of the contemporary socio-psychological ethos, Rushdie is concerned with an unimpassioned portrayal of the problem of alienation and does not bother to suggest any solution to it. His characters' problems are chiefly 'the everyday human problems which arise from character-and-environment' and their interplay (*Midnight's Children*, p. 238). These rootless persons are simply 'broken promises; made to be broken' (p. 523). What makes their lot even more pathetic is the fact that they have no choice but to face the music. Saleem asks :

> No choice ? —None ; when was there ever ?—There are imperatives and logical consequences, and inevitabilities, and recurrences ; there are things-done-to; and accidents, and blugeonings-of-fate ; when was there ever a choice ? When options ? When a decision freely-made, to be this or that or the other ? (pp. 503-504).

Rushdie's characters may not be heroic, but they faithfully represent the predicament which most modern people have to face today in one way or the other.

There is, moreover, a psychological validity behind Rushdie's delineation of rootlessness. The extent of temperamental and experiential identification between Indian novelists in English and their characters is really striking. "One strongly suspects", writes Meenakshi Mukherjee, "that is so because the novelists themselves, like their protagonists, feel alienated from these [i.e. Indian] values".[20] John Wain also finds them 'always haunted by a sense of loss and estrangement.'[21] Rushdie is no exception to this trend. In spite of his schooling at Rugby, his university years at Cambridge and his two-pronged rootlessness, he looks at his 'Indianness' in a nostalgiac way.[22] He has had a special affection for Bombay, where he was born and brought up and had his early education. The 'diseased reality' of his Pakistan years comes to his autobiographical hero Saleem 'like a terrible, occult series of reprisals for tearing up our Bombay roots' (p. 403). As is evident from *Shame*, Rushdie equates himself with 'all migrants' and has not managed to shake himself free of the idea of roots (pp. 87-88). He remarks : "I, too, know something of this immigrant business. I am an emigrant from one country (India) and a newcomer in two" (p. 85). This identification on the part of the novelist with his characters[23] gives verisimilitude to his work and makes his treatment of the dilemma of the alienated person so convincing.[24]

REFERENCES

1. S. Krishnan, *"Midnight's Children* : An Un-Indian Book on All Things Indian", *Aside* (April 1982), p. 53.
2. Salman Rushdie's interview with Gordon Wise, *Gentleman* (February 1984), p. 59.
3. *Ibid.* p. 57.
   For a detailed discussion, see R.S. Pathak, "History and the Individual in the Novels of Rushdie", in R.K. Dhawan (ed.), *Three Contemporary Novelists* (New Delhi : Classical Publishing Co., 1986).
4. *Studies in Indian English Literature* (New Delhi : Sterling, 1987), p. 54.
5. "Such Angst, Loneliness, Rootlessness", *Gentleman* (February 1984), p. 105.
6. See B. Murchland, *The Age of Alienation* (New York, 1971).
7. *Man in Modern Fiction* (New York : Random House, 1958), p. 3.
8. *The Spiritual Crisis of Man* (London : Rider & Co., 1972), p. 7.
9. "On the meaning of Alienation", *American Sociological Review* 24/6 (December 1959), p. 786.
10. I. Taviss, "Changes in the Form of Alienation". *American Sociological Review* 34/1 (February 1969), pp. 46-47.
11. M.D. Melwani, *Critical Essays on Indo-Anglian Themes.* (Calcutta 1971), p. 21.
12. Salman Rushdie, *Grimus* (Frogmore, St. Albans, Herts : Granada Publishing Limited, 1975), p. 220. All subsequent references to this novel are given parenthetically.

13. B.K. Joshi, "It may be Long, but it's Not Overwritten", *The Times of India* (1 November 1981), p. 8.
14. "*Midnight's Children* and Reader Responsibility", *Critical Quarterly* 26/3 (Autumn 1984), p. 33.
15. Salman Rushdie, *Midnight's Children* (New York : Avon Books, 1980), p. 3. Hereafter cited parenthetically.
16. Fernandez. *op. cit.*, p. 103.
17. Salman Rushdie, *Shame* (Calcutta : Rupa & Co., 1983), p. 173. Hereafter cited parenthetically.
18. Fernandez, *op. cit.*, p. 105.
19. *The Twice-Born Fiction* (New Delhi : Heinemann, 1972), p. 83.
20. *Ibid.*, p. 91.
21. "A Visit to India", *Encounter* 16/5 (May 1961), p. 7.
22. Rushdie told one of his reviewers : "The novel is in a crisis. . . . I cannot return to India. I don't feel like an Indian novelist". *The Times of India* (1 November 1981), p. 8.
In a different context, Rushdie is reported to have remarked : "Yes, the uprooting made me very sad. I was very angry when my parents sold our house [in Bombay] and Saleem Sinai, unable to forgive Karachi for not being Bombay, is very much like what I feel. . . . The novel [*Midnight's Children*] is written to sort of reclaim my roots, that part of my life. Yes, the writing of the book was a kind of high romantic way of paying a debt to India I felt I owed". *The Sunday Standard* (14 June 1981), p. 6.
23. In the interview given to Gordon Wise, Rushdie said that "the un-named narrator of *Shame* is a good deal closer to me than the named narrator of *Midnight's Children*". *Gentleman* (February 1984), p. 59. The identity between Saleem of *Midnight's Children* and its author, however, (including their names) is undeniable.
24. Rushdie's latest novel, *Satanic Verses* (Viking, 1988), has been banned in India, Egypt, Pakistan and South Africa. The novel has been called by the novelist his 'most serious book', which is 'also the most comic'. *India Today* (15 September 1988), p. 157. Rushdie regards his last three novels as parts of a triology. In an interview he told Shrabani Basu : "In this book [i.e. *The Satanic Verses*] I have, for the first time, managed to write from the whole of myself. . . . This book is a rounding off of a body of work that I have been engaged in for the last five years". *Sunday* (18-24 September 1988), p. 86.

16

Travelling with a Sunbeam : The Quest for Love and Identity

R. P. TEWARI

Kusum Ansal's *Travelling with a Sunbeam* is a novel with an apparent social purpose. It is feminist in essence, mild and mellow though, it presents a twilight view of love, marriage, sex and identity in the wake of the influence of the west on our traditional socio-cultural ethos. The novelist has sought to bring on the social horizon a hapless and loveless young woman who has in her the potential of a rebel. She has made an impassioned plea for the liberation of women's psyche submerged in the welter of our social moves grown moribund and meaningless. Shorn of ire and fire the novel presents a rather pathetic picture of a sensitive and sentimental young woman who finds herself in a precarious predicament consequent upon her mother's death and her father's re-marriage. As an expedient an alternative arrangement is made. She is kept away from her father and her new mummy so that she is no longer an irritant in the paradise of bliss promised by her father's second marriage.

As a result of the new arrangement, Surekha, a girl of four, is removed from the scene, and she starts living with her father's sister. No echo of Surekha's anguished cry is supposed to reach the vestibule of her father's new family set-up lest it should ruffle its peace and happiness. Bereaved of her mother and forsaken by her father, Surekha

embarks upon an uncertain voyage. She is led by an irony
of fate into a stagnant social lagoon cut off from the
main stream. She endeavours to get out of this lagoon
despite odds in her way.

Surekha's Bua mothers her. Although her Bua and her
husband have all the care and concern for her and bring
her up like their own child, Surekha never forgets that she
lost her mother soon after her birth. She "closely guarded
her secret feeling for her mother lest it (should) disappear
like the flickering smoke of a burning candle".[1] She continues to suffer from deprivations like a child who is wren-
ched from her parents' bosom and is dumped into another
family. What follows this makeshift arrangement forms the
nucleus of the story in the novel.

Surekha's life takes an uncertain and circuitous course
in the aftermath of her father's near-total unconcern and
her own feeling of alienation in her, Bua's family. Sensitive
as Surekha is, her forced expatriation tells upon her
emotional being. She tends to feel alone, unfriended and
melancholy. Her budding spirit is thwarted. Life becomes
boring and tedious and time hangs heavy on her. She feels
that she has been caught in a cobweb. The ambient
atomosphere casts a blight upon her. As a consequence,
she withdrawns into her insulated, private and personal
self. An aching chasm develops in her heart. She grows
into a lonely, loveless and uncared for woman though she
tries not to betray her loneliness and ennui. Notwithstanding her adverse circumstances she does not suffer
atrophy. Her heart still throbs with love and her ego seeks
a distinct identity. The feminine urge in her is neither
paralysed nor anaesthetised inside her. She grows within
herself into a full woman waiting for an opportunity to
burst into efflorescence.

Surekha gets everything in her Bua's house — love,
care and comfort, but consciously or unconsciously "the
feeling of something waithing here took deep root in her
and she finds that "her presence in the house was inciden-
tal". In spite of the fact that she is uprooted she tries to
retain her inner confidence that she has got "to achieve

something in life" (p. 12). She hates "the tribe of bridegroom sought for her". The comments of the bridegroom's side -- "Her Mummy is so fair and pretty ! Did she eat brinjal and dark Jamuns before the birth of her daughter" (p. 13) — are not only typical in our society but are like sprinkling of salt over her green wounds.

She is not welcome in her own father's house. She has to face her step-mother's wrath when she returns home. Though beautiful her mother in anger looks "horrid, a perfect Durga or Chandi in the battlefield". (p. 14). In her sub-conscious mind the mother is probably envious of her daughter—the fact that she has usurped her filial rights seems to haunt her or her step-daughter is a fly in the ointment.

Surekha's deprivation manifests itself in a variety of ways. She maintains a facade of tranquillity like a placid stream but conceals beneath her tranquillity a seething strife. There surges a wave of passion struggling to reach the shore. She is torn between desire and diffidence. She thirsts for love on the one hand and quests for identity on the other. Her exhibition in the marriage-market fills her with indignation and disgust so much so that she comes to detest the very idea of marriage, which to her means becoming a man's goods and chattels. To her marriage of this sort is nothing short of "a post mortem of her sentiments" and this "surgery tears her to bits and pieces" (p. 12). If marriage means all this, she would prefer to throw off the yoke of marriage.

In this atmosphere of seeming love; Surekha thirsts for love, love that flows from the heart uncontaminated by hypocrisy and selfishness. But because of her inhibiting circumstances she does not display her real self. As a result, her love remains unspelt and inarticulate for quite some time. But her inner self is aflame with love and responsive to every breeze that blows. She offers herself fully and spontaneously to Prashant's gesture of love. The passion of love imprisoned in her heart bursts out with exuberance: "Surekha's entire body was electrified, as though a mild current was flowing from Prashant into her" (p. 17). She wanted "to identify and give a name to the quiet moment just gone by." (p. 17). She desired to know for definite "the meaning of that touch that really gave her something," (p. 17) She felt convinced that "the embrace of the arms and the touch of the lips did signify to her that she was not absolutely "unwanted", she, too, did matter "somewhat", and was indeed "something".

This is the first instance of the recognition of her individuality and the realization of the woman in her. Her feeling that she is loved by someone fills her with rapture, though the blessed feeling lasts a moment only. This gives her not only a thrill of delight but a gleam of hope. This goes a long way to ward off frustration creeping in upon her. She has another chance encounter with Prashant in the train. She encourages him to take full liberties with her, but not in the real sense of accepting him or offering herself to him. It has a limited purpose. She wants him "to arouse her dormant sentiments—and provoke her feelings" (p. 25). Perhaps such a touch was needed by her to keep the woman in her alive and vibrant.

Surekha gets a first in Law but to find a "good groom" in her business community is a problem. She met with rejection and humiliation. She is compelled to wander "in a wild forest and confront insects, sadness, loneliness with her shattered dreams" (p. 28). She performs her domestic chores unconcernedly like an automation. Her heart is somewhere else. To top it all, "the sadistic aspect" of her stepmother's personality adds to her misery and despair. Her father, though helpless, is the only source of solace and support.

Surekha's agony is augmented when she sees offensive contrasts around her. Her cousin lives in a college hostel in Delhi. She wears "hot pants", swims in a bikini in the Club pool, "dates" and is a "vamp". But her mother has the check to deliver sermons to the simple Surekha on simplicity, modesty, morality and the like. Then there is Madhur, Surekha's friend, a college lecturer, living a bohemian life. She has never known love despite her affairs galore. To her "love is nothing beyond sex" (p. 33). Her philosophy of life is "to shovel her way forward" (p. 33).

But in spite of those distractions Surekha ploughs her way up. Her love for Shiva Kaushik, a lawyer by profession, is something like love at first sight. Her inarticulate love and suppressed ego find their clear articulation when she comes into contact with him as his junior. She is instinctively and irresistibly drawn towards him. He is a middle-aged man and married with a grown-up son. He is unhappily married. He and his wife "move on two parallel tracks — both are temperamentally poles apart" (p. 39). Shiva is "very much an Indian" while his wife Manjari is totally steeped "in the western outlook"—ultra-modern. She wears western clothes and is a chain smoker. She suffers from a "film-fixation". She is "sick a sadist". She even "beats up" Shiva. On the contrary, Shiva is always calm and serious. He needed "a very simple", "a very affectionate, very loving type of a wife who could bring the angel out of the man." (p. 39). They are husband and wife only in name. Though living under the same roof, they are too far off from each other. Their house is a battle-field between belligerent wife and pacifist husband.

Surekha is enchanted by Shiva. She determines to achieve his love. In Shiva and through Shiva, she seems to find an answer—indeed a right answer—to the stirrings of her heart and recognition of her identity. Married though, Shiva longs for love, love that flows from the heart, love that only a woman like Surekha could give. Surekha too, yearns for love. Shiva's life, love of a married man, a man who is ill-yoked in marriage. She feels that she can fill his heart with love and he can fill hers. For Shiva's love, she refuses Prashant's "inviting hands and also his rising affection and passion for her" (p. 44). She also refuses the love of Shiva's son. The new spell created by Shiva is "hazy and acrid like smoke, yet she was dying to wrap it around him" (p. 44). When she saw him, "she felt totally dissolving herself in him" (p. 44). The woman in her with all her fulness and fervour was only too willing to burst at the seams.

Shiva symbolises for Surekha everything—a sculptor, a painter, a poet, an author and what not. Her supreme interest in Shiva. She desires "to stir him into action, into ebullience so as to make him rise and engulf the entire house with the melody of waves" (p. 51). In this marriage of true minds love finds its consummate fulfilment far removed from the sanctimonious bonds of wedlock. Shiva's "intense thirst is quenched" in his consummation with Surekha, and Surekha, too, becomes "unconscious" in those moments of ecstasy and "floats" in the sea of happiness. Her firm resolve is not to be a burden, a burden, that people like to be "dumped into the matrimonial palanquin and be done with" (p. 85). She determines to carve out her own career. She would not like to get into a rut and marry a social and financial parasite. Though Shiva and Surekha cannot live together, they are happy and their love goes far beyond the bonds and sanctions of matrimony. Their sincere love sanctifies their relationship though it is illicit from a myopic point of view. It explodes the myth of conjugal sanctimony. It is a counterblast to the institution of marriage idolised and glorified as a sacrament and spiritual union. Here is a union of loving hearts rather than the ritual of marriage devoid of love. Love is the true test of morality and the rest is not germane to the issue.

Surekha loses her indentity in Shiva's for her total fulfilment. Manjari calls her a fool for having lost her heart to a middle-aged man. But Surekha's real adviser is her own heart. The word marriage has absolutely no sanctity for her. She has known the great humbug that marriage is in most cases. Her father is dominated by her Mummy. Shiva and Manjari live like "two opposite magnetic poles". Minna's life wretched. She finds that "in today's modern and educated families, where you expect refinement and understanding, you are confronted with a gang of greedy thugs where girls such as my sister are suffocated to death" (p. 114).

The "complex and crammed life" of Surekha is revitalized by Shiva's love. Addressing Shiva's photograph, Surekha says, "I am an ordinary sentimental woman; under my rough exterior of a very busy person, there lies a tender heart which pulsates with emotion....... Shiva's personality touches my soft chords even in the midst of my preoccupations" (p. 117). Here we find absolute surrender of one throbbing heart to another throbbing heart. It is an irony indeed that Shiva is lonely, Madhur is lonely, Minna is lonely. Surekha asks, ''What is marriage a substitute for one's loneliness?'' (p. 118). But in Surekha, though outside wedlock, Shiva gets everything—that pleasure of life which Manjari could never give him. Shiva's love changes the very fabric of Surekha's life. Minna's unnatural death fills Surekha's heart with disgust. She comes to develop an aversion to marriage. She bursts out in a paroxysm of anger : "Marriage—marriage ? Have you lost your head, Madhur, you, telling me all this ? You, who helped me to believe that one could also do without marriage ? Tied to her matrimonial knot, my Minna, my poor Minna is gone now, gone forever" (p. 137).

It can be seen that Surekha, through her life of tribulation and revolt, heralds the advent of "The new woman", questing and struggling for love and identity. Kusum Ansal's social conscience does not luxuriate in the cloud-cuckoo-land of sterile idealism. The ideal woman seems to have died with Cordelia :

"Her voice was ever soft,
Gentle and low—an excellent thing in woman".
                    (*King Lear*, Act V, Sc. III, LL. 273-74)

Surekha symbolises the birth of "the new woman" who is conscious of her identity and is eager for social recognition and status. She represents nascent feminism which has vast potential to grow and develop in our hidebound society. She articulates, though not very militantly and vigorously, the resurgence of feminist feelings. She does not speak with suffragette eloquence and suffers greatly the agony of social constraints and moral inhibitions. However, in spite of odds, she strives to attain her individual identity so as to able to shape her own destiny. She doss not isolate or ostracise herself but struggles to find a firm footing for herself.

Surekha maintains her individuality. She merges her identity only when she finds perfect fulfilment of herself in a man like Shiva. The institution of marriage, as it exists today, is like a rotten apple with an unblemished skin. It merely maintains a facade of righteousness. The novelist has ventured to strip away the veil of romantic haze from the not-all-lovely face of what is sanctified and adored as wedlock. Shelley is uncompromising when he says, "A husband and wife ought to continue so long united as they love each other : any law that should bind them to cohabitation for one moment after the decay of their affection would be the most intolerable tyranny and most unworthy of toleration."

(Notes on "Queen Mab").

Kusum Ansal, through this novel, makes a powerful plea for the liberation of both men and women from the slavery of every kind, social, moral and sexual. Surekha is not a fullgrown, militant feminist. Hers is nascent feminism, pleading for women's right to love and identity. This is the cry of her heart.

REFERENCES

1. Kusum Ansal, *Travelling with a Sunbeam*, New Delhi : Vikas Publishing House Pvt. Ltd., 1983, p. 10.

All subsequent references to this work are given parenthetically.

17

V. A. Shahane's Doctor Fauste : A Novel of Reality Resurrection

It was Johann Spies who first initiated the Faust myth by publishing *Faustbuch* in 1587. It has since made its appearance in a variety of interpretations and significance at various intervals of time and space in the works of Christopher Marlowe, and Thomas Mann. But it had never crossed the continent. It is for the first time that it has appeared in the east in *Doctor Fauste*, a novel by V. A. Shahane. The title page declares the novel to be "An Indian Version of the Legend of Faustus". Though the basic core of the legend can be reduced to the framework of bartering soul to the devil in the pursuit of power and passion, the legend has been variously adopted to suit the requirements of different times and countries, thus sifting its elements and aspects in a varying emphasis. The recreation of the Faust myth by V. A. Shahane, therefore, may be seen not in its theoretical framework but in what it seeks to render through its mythical potential.

What this novel happens to focus upon is the way 'reality' is lost track of in the fancied pursuit of dreams and desires by the innocent youngmen of modern India. A close study of this novel's text would show that in the Indian version of Doctor Fauste, that is, of Trivikram Tukaram Fauste, the pursuit of power was not abstract but "was indeed one of the mysteries of my growing' into boyhood and youth".[1] The totality of the nature and texture of this growing into boyhood and youth very much depended upon the kind of atmosphere and environment one grew into. What Shahane, therefore, characterises in the novel is the making of a Fauste and the recreation and enacting of the Fauste myth on the Indian soil—" a funny reincarnation of the Western man on eastern soil" (p. 11). The sun-dial image here suggests that what happened in the west could also happen in the east.

The basic problem in the growth of Tivi is his 'intellect'. As he says, "I'm an abstract thinker. I am searching for a subject which will satisfy my inner cravings" (p. 14). And his 'inner cravings' are for "A world of profit and delight, of power and honour, of intense sex and spirituality—in short, of pure ecstacy..." which he wants to achieve through "Modern magic ! Modern tantra ! Modern Kundalini yoga ! Pure ancient Indian art mixed with modern western science" (p. 14). The young Tivi makes it so because all around him in India there is a whole religious culture of magic pedalled by the so-called Sadhus and Saints of today. "Papa Paropkari has already promised to initiate me into the world of magic" (p. 15). He makes it a deliberate choice because he is aware of the sinister hook-up of religion with politics in the power game in the country. He, therefore, rightly says that "We can buy political power with it, and finance the entire election machinery of many socalled democratic parties". (p. 16). Both religion and politics, today, are being held before the people not as righteous conduct but as flippant behaviour. Tivi, therefore, reflects that "I'm Fauste pure and simple. I want power and pleasure—I'm the new young man of modern India—a true Indian yuppie" (p.16).

From the above analysis it becomes clear that Fauste 'pure and simple' is desire for power and pleasure, which characterises growing in boyhood and youth. The novelist here is not concerned with the legendary or mythical Fauste but with the archetype which could be discovered in all lands and times for profit. The diary of Tivi is a brilliant record of the making of a Fauste in modern India. Trivikram Tukaram Fauste was a brilliant and active College student. He was "the centre of all attention, like a statue on an island in the lake. Everyone admired him, his zest, his courage, his dare-devilry. He was the darling and heart throb of many college girls" (p. 25). He also contested the college elections.

The scene at Tivi's College election was rather different from such similar situations in the past. For many years College elections were just fun, a play-house of small tricks and girl-hunting, gaiety and graffiti. Now the whole scene had altered. Political parties of all hue were pouring money into college elections and preparing the future citizens for the devious game of actual power politics, the chess-board of power (p. 26).

Tivi, under the given Indian scene, thought of himself 'as greater than that legendary Faustus' and "dreamt that his range was even wider and deeper than Faustus's, and that he was a man of destiny who would control the *tribhuvan*...a *gagan-bhedi*, a god-defier, a new *avtar*, a new incarnation of the energy of the earth" (p. 27). He, therefore, "disapproved of the implications of the old-fashioned—now an archaic god—*Prajapati* as he thought of him as no longer useful to the modern world of 1986—the India of 1986" (p. 27). He even dismissed the image of the whole Hindu cosmos of Prajapati, Brahma, Vishnu and Shiva from his mind as quite irrelevant to the human condition, and in its place he substituted new gods—gods of power and wealth, earthly grandeur and sensual pleasure ! He thought of Gandhi Caps and Nehru *Kurtas*, Khaddar dhotis and Kolhapuri *Chappals* as "the true embodiment of power in the India of 1986" (p. 27). For his victory in his college elections, he thought that it was all due to the blessings of Papa Paropkari—"the almighty magician—sage ! The real power behind this event." (p. 28). By now Tivi has bartered away his soul to Lucifer-Ravana in exchange of a life of pleasure and power lasting for twenty-for months. It is appropriately that the Personal Assistant to the Chief Minister, Syed Abdul Karim, appears on the scene as Marich Mephistopheles to request Tivi to invest his "soul into his political faction, and support him all through !

Mobilise all the student leaders for his election campaign" and then "He will put money in your purse! You may enjoy life for twenty-four months, or as long as the Sahib is in his saddle" (p. 30).

This is how magic merges religion with politics as a potent medium of exploitation of the innocent masses and youngmen in India today. Tivi's love for magic as a source of power, therefore, finds a parallel in the world outside him. His untutored growing needs find a good breeding ground in the milieu, Besides the fact that in the male-female bio-psychological tangle women have always been looked upon as symbols of sex, Tivi' desire and attraction for women is a natural aspect of his growth as a young-man. He, therefore, dreams of girls as things to enjoy and conquer and has affairs, both with the sensuous Sushila and the protective Suniti. In his Ashram, Papa Paropkari informs Tivi.

"You must follow the tantric code and all the tan-tric rites. You must give yourself away—to my pretty ashramite girls—Let yourself go—allow the girls to have a go .... Follow meticulously the *tantric* postures and poses—drink the divine nectar—and the eternal woman would arouse the *Kundalini* in you—pure sex is neither vulgar not obscene. It's the true gateway to god and magic (p. 43).

Since Tivi was an incurable romantic, a dreamer and an over-reacher, he took Papa Paropkari's teachings to be as real as he took his own airy notions and fancies to be reality. He felt greatly enamoured of all the agents of power in religion, politics and sex. But his spell is broken by the appearance of Suniti in the Ashram, who sees him to be "A victim of the illusions of power and knowledge, and of mere animal enjoyment" and urges upon him to "Try to be a man, try to be human" (p. 48) and "to under-stand the real and the factual world" (p. 47).

Suniti, therefore, takes him to a genuine saint, Swami Satishchandra of Sri Ramakrishna Ashram, who tries to dispel many of his illusions and his lure for power and magic. Though Swamiji describes all political, money or sex power to be "part of maya" he regards it as "very much factual" and "important for realising the truth of an inexplicable object." (p. 51). Swamiji explodes the illusion of magic and mastering *Siddhis* to control the world by saying that "There is no magic in this world except that which is reflected in love" and that one can "control the world only through love and altruistic action" (p. 52). He, therefore, advises Tivi to "Follow the path of dedicated service to mankind, to the poor and needy in India. Try to purify public life and our present value—system" (p. 52). Thereupon, Suniti takes Tivi to the red-light area to show what reality and life is like. When the gruesome tale of Zeenat's life came to light, "Trivikram Fauste, who lived in the dreamy world of 'self' was violently shaken by this painful story—a glimpse, as Suniti said, into an aspect of 'real life'." (p. 57).

Suniti further takes him to "almost another world, a little hamlet in the heart of native, rural grassroot India .. a kind of search for 'real' India" to rescue him "from the overpowering spell of the mysterious magic', which came to him in the form of temptations of a highly corrupt world, of both spirit and matter...from Marich Mephistophilis' firm grip . . . and other forms of exploitation indulged in by the new satans of modern India" (p. 61). There Tivi meets an illiterate woman Narsamma who narrates to him the tale of exploitation of her family by the Zamindar and the way she took personal revenge upon him to avenge the death of her husband even at the risk of losing her young son, untraced so far. In his meeting with Zeenat, arranged for his sensual pleasures by Marich Mephistophilis, Tivi informs about what he is pledged to do and receive in return for his services to Marich. "I've to act his election agent, especially among grown-up students and youthgroups in Colleges and Universities. I've to arrange invitations for him for inaugurating student's unions and youth camps and youth festivals and things like that" (p. 75).

He hopes to get some reward in return :

I can get permits, quotas, licences, and I can distribute favours. I can offer the tainted gold...I can depute people to conferences in Moscow and Toronto, even to Las Vegas! Abdul Karim likes pretty girls, and surprisingly those high society women, like him too'. This suits both of us and we have a good time...But more important than everything in this world is access to money, I can write cheques and they're honoured by his banks, Indian and foreign banks, Swiss banks too! (p. 75).

Thus, Tivi inadvertently exposes the corruption rampant in our country. The charges of grave misuse of power and misappropriation, of both public and state fauds, against the Chief Minister, Syed Abdul Karim, in the Court by plaintiff Gopal Kale "had taken the lid off a very large reservoir of corruption that was modern political India" (p. 87). It had been pointed out by the plaintiff in the Court how "the higher-ups in Delhi, too, were party to these deals and frauds" (p. 88). But the greatest shock to Tivi comes when Anita, a girl once introduced to him for a gay-time, appears as a pious Khadi Clad social worker in the court to testify "Syed Abdul Karim's excellent moral character, his honesty and his deep devotion to Indian values" (p. 90). After the Court scene, the worst of it is discovered by Tivi in Anita's bedroom, where she is seen lying naked with Syed Abdul Karim.

From now onwards Tivi felt a kind of change coming over him. "He then fancied he was face to face with the Truth of Being implicit in the Cosmos and the Great Globe itself! In such rare moments he thought he saw a new Reality—the Reality that is at once human and divine." (p. 94). Sushila at this moment, seemed to him to be the only person to turn to, who could save him and his soul from the inevitable tragic doom. But soon the spell is broken when Sushila, his would-be-bride, is not only discovered semi-nude in the bed of Papa Paropkari but also married to Manik Budhwar, a one-time class fellow of Tivi, a college-tough, lover, mischief-maker, election agent, moneyspinner all in one and now a Junior Minister of State in the Government. Though this betrayal dazed and stunned Tivi, it "made him see within himself and it gave him a new awareness, fresh areas of insight, new horizons of hope and faith" (p. 105). He discovered how "For years, Fauste had behaved like a sceptic, an agnostic, an atheist, and a curious 'believer in no belief.' He had parroted *Charvaka* they said, and also *The Book of Job*, and many other texts of spiritual unbelief. He was an Anglophile as well as an irrepressible rebel. He had allowed himself to be proudly and shamelessly fed on foreign intellectual fare" (p. 107), which had made him, what Suniti called, 'a bundle of contradictions, a paradoxical puzzle.' But how the tide had turned. He was now feeling in his veins 'a subtle undercurrent of the call of the divine' and a deep devotion for the principal deities and sacred places of Maharashtra Vithoba at Pandharpur, Shri Mahalaxmi at Kolhapur and Tulja Bhawani at Tuljapur. And, when he bathed in the Chandrabhaga, "he had a feeling of being baptised anew. The strange currents gave him an awareness of the mystery of existence and of the subleties of the Hindu faith" (p. 109). That is why "Being rational, he thought, doesn't solve life's complex problems" (p. 113). He, therefore, returns to Suniti, the symbol of wisdom. But, perhaps, it was too late. The period of contract with Marich Mephistophilis was over. Besides, he had flouted 'the all-important condition not to utter the name of God.' The Yama-dutas from Lucifer had arrived to claim his soul. Fauste had been admitted to a clinic, where he died of cardiac failure.

Thus three factors combine to create the Fauste in Tivi —his young age innocent fancies and passions, his intellectual training in Western thought, knowledge and rationality and, the socio-political corruption around in the country. All these put together displace Tivi's focus and apprehension of reality and make him run after fancies for truth and illusions for reality. His sub-conscious, therefore, becomes a playground of paradoxical fancies and sensations. He loses the sense of wholeness of life and sees life in fractions. He becomes a dreamor, a fantasist and, above all, a foolish ego-pusher, assuming all kinds of roles for himself. His western education makes him a prig,

a sceptic, a rebel and a god-defier of a type. The worst of
it was that he was a being all these in a vacuum,
where there was neither the west to react nor the
east to live with. He thus, becomes alienated from
his self, roots and contexts and pursues erratic cravings
after authority and sensuality. And for all this he wants
to find an easy way out in *tantra* or magic, throwing to the
winds the logic of labour and result, ends and means, sincerity and attainments. In short, he becomes an incorrigi-
ble prey of illusions which he pursues like reality. It is at
this stage and in such a situation that he falls into the trap
of the agents of corruption in religion, society and politics. Whether in the exercise of one's innocence or forced
self-delusions, once a youngman in India is ready to pursue his cravings, the corrupt environment around is too
ready to offer him fertile grounds for damnation for its own
ends.

What V.A. Shahane is trying to do in this novel is not
to create the Faust-myth in terms of the western suppo-
sitions and background but represent the essence of the
spirit and concept of Faust manifesting itself beyond the
confines of time, space and culture. Since the novel traces
in a well calculated manner the emergence and the making
of the Faust in India, it is only proper that his illusions are
set right against the very realities which are India today.
There are two observable levels of realities in today's India—
one which controls and rules the masses from without, and
the second which pervades and sustains the masses from
within. To say it in other words, one level is observed via
the west and intellect, while the second is felt via the
senses and the organicity of being a part of ancient heritage. The Faustian elements and spirit in Tivi become
concretised when his inner temptations get easy opportunities for fulfilment and his illusions are comfortably
matched with the external realities. The ruling power game
and machinery in Indian politics today has become a safe
ground for the promotion of the Faust-spirit in the country. The displacement brought about by the western education and culture has further strengthened and multiplied

the evil in the country. The mental focus of the Indian youth has been distorted and imagination diseased. The youth today is not only full of illusions but self-delusive enough to permit exploitation by power mongers. The situation they find themselves in is both critical and frustrating. They have been alienated both from their self and the realities of their country. The bonds have been broken.

How to connect, then, is the problem ? How to ressurrect reality is the issue ? The novelist 'adopts two ways of resolving the tangle for Tivi. First, the surfaces the hypocrisy, pretence, immorality and corruption underlying the manoeuvrings of the religious and political leaders in the country today. Secondly, he reveals different aspects of reality and real India to bring about a change in focus of perception of Tivi. As Suniti tells Tivi, "The real India you'll see only when you meet people—poor people living in our villages, ill-clad, ill-fed, ill-housed—very poor indeed, who have a heart of gold which would put a millionaire to shame ! These are the 'discarded' of our civilization, the unfortunates, the unlucky victims of fate and also of an unjust social system !" (p. 62). When Tivi's subjective world is face to face with the objective one, a new sense of reality dawns on him through a progressive dismantling of illusions about himself and the world outside.

Tivi discovers that his illusions are as sick and rotten as the society and culture outside him. The resurrection of reality first begins at home. He then realises the reality of both the present and past, the seeming and the real India and his place and relationship with them. He learns that his egotism and primal alienation had reduced him to a demonic self-encapsulation rendering him susceptible to an irrational and erratic play of fantasies and illusions. He also comes to understand that what can be played out in fantasy and imagination cannot be acted out in life without some damnation of soul. Doctor Fauste thus resurrects the lost conscience and the need to adhere to morality and ethics in personal conduct and human relationships. Sympathy for the victims of injustice and the poor neglected masses in India is restored. The sense of continuity and presentness of the past as part of Indian reality is re-established in the psyche of Tivi. The imaginative content of Indian reality, which is an admixture of dirt-disorder and spirituality—harmony, is recreated. The bearings of revolt and defiance against God are changed to surrender and faith. Incessant mental questionings and sensual cravings are silenced in the union of the self with the divine in mankind. Contrasting the personal fantasies with the living socio-political realities around, Doctor Fauste returns to the true nature of reality. The struggle thus redresses the cultural impoverishment of the present India.

Though, like Italo Calvino's *Cosmicomics*, Shahane keeps one foot in the myth and another in reality, he uses the myth more for subversive purposes—first, to explode the myth of freedom and advancement of modern India, and secondly, to expose the selling and bartering of the soul of the entire new generation of Satan in the country. It is this function which informs the basic structure of the novel. It is precisely this which makes it an Indian version of the legend of Faustus. And that is why Tivi does not come out as great a heroic figure as one of those western Faustuses. Instead, like Ken Casey's *One Flew Over the Cuckoo's Nest*, Shahane symbolizes in him as the minor representative of a larger conspiracy and corruption. Once Tivi has colluded with the forces of corruption and bartered his soul to the Devil, there can be no pity or forgiveness for his misadventures. There can only be a struggle for the resurrection of reality and a resolute will to fight whatever frustrates its realization. That is why the drop of rain on the bilva leaf "symbolized Trivikram Fauste's indomitable spirit and will to fight against his fate" (p. 121). The evil has to be fought out both internally and externally and both made compatible and livable. The resurrection of reality on the level of the self 'can' be obtained by overcoming illusions and, on the level of external world or India, by reaching out to the poor masses and the ancient heritage of the country.

Doctor Fauste of Shahane is different in its use and application of the Faust myth in yet another way. Unlike the

Christian and Western philosophy of Satan,sin and temptation, it is based on the philosophy of illusions and *maya*. No
grace from outside can interfere the scheme here. Tivi has
to resurrect the lost reality all by himself and die in the
knowledge of its realisation on a larger level of existence.
That is why the transcendence and liberation, denied to the
hero of Christopher Marlowe, is available to him. Tivi,
by re-locating himself and his place in the history and
culture and the present and past of India, bridges the gap
between the self and the non-self and opens up the possibility of redemption and resurrection in the space-time
continuum of the people and the land.

REFERENCES

1. V.A. Shahane, *Doctor Fauste* (New Delhi : Arnold-Heinemann,
1986), p. 11.
All subsequent references are given parenthetically.

INDEX

Ever since its inception, the Indian fiction in English has grown considerably in bulk, variety and maturity, and, as Mulk Raj Anand says, it has 'come to stay as part of world literature'. On account of historical reasons, however, the Indian novelist in English has to face unprecedented challenges arising out of his quest for and assertion of identity and the choice of medium. The present volume, containing seventeen essays by eminent scholars, discusses the problems and promises of the Indian fiction in English in considerable detail. The novelists included for analysis are : Mulk Raj Anand, R. K. Narayan, Raja Rao, K. A. Abbas, Kamala Markandaya, R. P. Jhabvala, Nayantara Sahgal, Anita Desai, Arun Joshi, Shashi Deshpande, Salman Rushdie, Kusum Ansal and V. A. Shahane.

Dr R .S. Pathak is Professor and Head of the Department of English and other European Languages at Dr Harisingh Gour Vishwavidyalaya (formerly University of Saugar), Sagar, India. He was awarded Ph.D. in 1971 and D.Litt. in 1986 by the University of Saugar. He also holds a Postgraduate Diploma in the Teaching of English from the Central Institute of English and Foreign Languages, Hyderabad and a Master's degree in English as a Second Language from the University of Wales.

Dr Pathak has contributed many papers to prestigious journals. He has also published five books – Oscar Wilde : A Critical Study (1976), The Phonetics of Bagheli (1980), Oblique Poetry in Indian and Western Poetics (1988), Vakrokti and Stylistics (1988) and Poetic and Non-Poetic Discourse (1989).